Contents

Introduction

TERRORISM is Volume 355 in the **ISSUES** series. The aim of the series is to offer current, diverse information about important issues in our world, from a UK perspective.

ABOUT TERRORISM

Sadly, terrorism is an ever-present feature in the news and it can be an upsetting and controversial topic to discuss. In this book we look at different terrorist groups, the growing threat of far-right violent extremism, radicalisation and current counter-terrorism strategies.

OUR SOURCES

Titles in the **ISSUES** series are designed to function as educational resource books, providing a balanced overview of a specific subject.

The information in our books is comprised of facts, articles and opinions from many different sources, including:

- Newspaper reports and opinion pieces
- Website factsheets
- Magazine and journal articles
- Statistics and surveys
- Government reports
- Literature from special interest groups.

A NOTE ON CRITICAL EVALUATION

Because the information reprinted here is from a number of different sources, readers should bear in mind the origin of the text and whether the source is likely to have a particular bias when presenting information (or when conducting their research). It is hoped that, as you read about the many aspects of the issues explored in this book, you will critically evaluate the information presented.

It is important that you decide whether you are being presented with facts or opinions. Does the writer give a biased or unbiased report? If an opinion is being expressed, do you agree with the writer? Is there potential bias to the 'facts' or statistics behind an article?

ASSIGNMENTS

In the back of this book, you will find a selection of assignments designed to help you engage with the articles you have been reading and to explore your own opinions. Some tasks will take longer than others and there is a mixture of design, writing and research-based activities that you can complete alone or in a group.

FURTHER RESEARCH

At the end of each article we have listed its source and a website that you can visit if you would like to conduct your own research. Please remember to critically evaluate any sources that you consult and consider whether the information you are viewing is accurate and unbiased.

Useful websites

www.adl.org

www.capx.co

www.delta-net.com

www.economicsandpeace.org

www.educare.co.uk.

www.esrc.ukri.org

www.europol.europa.eu

www.gov.uk

www.henryjacksonsociety.org

www.hopenothate.org.uk

www.inews.co.uk

www.mi5.gov.uk

www.news-decoder.com

www.ons.gov.uk

www.parliament.uk

www.politico.eu

www.pressassociation.com

www.rightsinfo.org

www.theconversation.com

www.theecologist.org

www.theguardian.com

www.theweek.co.uk

www.visionofhumanity.org

Terrorism

Editor: Tracy Biram

Volume 355

Independence Educational Publishers

First published by Independence Educational Publishers

The Studio, High Green

Great Shelford

Cambridge CB22 5EG

England

© Independence 2019

Copyright

Photocopy licence

ISBN-13: 978 1 86168 811 8

Printed in Great Britain

Zenith Print Group

Decoder: What is terrorism? And who are terrorists?

A bloody attack in New Zealand brought the word "terrorist" back into the headlines. What is terrorism, and why is the term controversial?

By Tom Heneghan

'One man's terrorist is another man's freedom fighter' is one of those warnings journalists often hear from editors when they report about political violence.

Terms like "terrorism" or "terrorist" are highly charged, and using them in a specific case can put a journalist on one side of a controversy. That's because they imply criticism of the goal of the attack, and there may be two or more sides to the story.

So while terror is undeniably a factor in much of the political violence of recent decades, using terror-related terms can be tricky. Editors sometimes advise reporters to use descriptions like "militant" or "urban guerrilla" to get around the problem.

Let's pick apart the problem of terrorism to understand why the term is so fraught.

What is terrorism?

In the abstract, terrorism is the use of indiscriminate violence to strike fear in the public's mind in pursuit of a political aim. Concretely, that could be an aeroplane crashing into a skyscraper, a bomb in a crowded marketplace, a gun attack in a house of prayer or the assassination of a leader.

The problem arises with the purpose of the violence. Attackers' goals can be ousting the people in power, setting up a new type of state or simply creating chaos to undermine the establishment in any given society.

By definition, attackers believe their cause is just. Their supporters would see them as freedom fighters. Those who are targeted – both the innocent victims and the authority under siege – would denounce the attackers as terrorists.

'Attackers believe their cause is just.'

Note that our definition stresses the violence is indiscriminate. Terror assaults are usually a surprise attack in which little or no effort is made to avoid killing innocent bystanders.

Traditionally, armies fight armies and enemy soldiers are considered to be valid targets. Shoppers at a market or a controversial politician are not supposed to be fair game.

Who are the terrorists?

Terrorism, on the other hand, is an equal-opportunity strategy. It is relatively easy to organise, so no one political, ethnic or religious group has a monopoly on it.

Just reading the headlines in many Western newspapers might give a different impression. Many terror attacks in the past few decades have been staged by radical Muslims. Many of these seem to have their roots in the turbulent politics of the Muslim world.

But not all terrorists are Muslim, and virtually all Muslims are not terrorists. Several shooting sprees in recent years have been the work of white supremacists or other groups involving no Muslims.

'No one group has a monopoly on terrorism'

Australian Brenton Tarrant killed 50 worshippers in two mosques in New Zealand last week, American Dylann Roof murdered nine African-Americans in South Carolina in 2015 and Norwegian Anders Behring Brevik shot dead 77 people in Oslo at a socialist summer camp.

Tamil Tigers from Sri Lanka's Hindu minority used suicide bombers during that country's 26-year civil war, which ended in 2009.

Indiscriminate violence has been used by both sides in the Israeli-Palestinian conflict.

Buddhism is known as a peaceful religion, but there are Buddhist monks in Myanmar, Thailand and Sri Lanka whose inflammatory sermons advocate ethnic cleansing by the military.

Why opt for terrorism?

Terrorism can be the nuclear weapon of the weaker party in a conflict. Armies and police forces are supposed to follow rules of engagement, which can limit their options because they are charged with avoiding innocent victims.

Ignoring those rules allows terrorists to attack anywhere at any time. This strikes fear among the public and tempts armies or police forces to respond in kind. If they do, they can become discredited in the eyes of the public.

It also empowers so-called non-state actors, which are movements or even individuals who can challenge a sovereign state. The ancient Chinese strategist Sun Tzu laid out a cardinal rule for any military: "Know your enemy." But terrorism is only a strategy, or a means to an end, so it confounds generals trained to look for an enemy to fight.

'Terrorists ignore traditional rules of engagement.'

We've been making the distinction here between established armies and freelance terrorists, but in practice it's not so clear. Sometimes states operate according to accepted rules in public, but also support violent covert operations meant to destabilise other states or groups.

For example, radical Muslims fighting to take power in the Indian state of Kashmir have long operated from inside neighbouring Pakistan. Islamabad denies it supports them but is conspicuously lax when calls to crack down on these militants come from India and other countries, including the United States and Britain.

Terrorists or freedom fighters?

Terrorists can also morph into freedom fighters when their violent cause evolves into a movement that others come to see as justified.

Nelson Mandela, South Africa's first black president, is widely considered today as a healer who helped reconcile whites and blacks in the 1990s after his country scrapped its racist policy of apartheid.

In his younger years, however, Mandela and his African National Congress approved an underground bombing campaign against white rule. The United States put them on its terrorist watch list in 1988 and didn't remove them until 20 years later.

'Mandela was once considered a terrorist.'

In 1993, the Norwegian Nobel Committee awarded Mandela its annual Peace Prize along with white President Frederik Willem de Klerk 'for their work for the peaceful termination of the apartheid regime, and for laying the foundations for a new democratic South Africa.'

The following year, Palestinian Liberation Organization leader Yasser Arafat won the Peace Prize along with Israeli Prime Minister Yitzhak Rabin and Israeli Foreign Minister Shimon Peres for signing the Oslo peace accords.

"Arafat won the Nobel Peace Prize."

In his early years, Arafat was so identified with radical tactics that the Nobel Committee wrote that "Palestinian guerrilla groups … resorted to terror to attract world attention, but it gradually became clear to Arafat that he would have to accept the state of Israel for the USA to be willing to mediate in the dispute."

Gerry Adams, an Irish republican leader in Northern Ireland, has been identified by opponents and former allies alike as a commander in the outlawed Irish Republican Army that bombed and attacked British soldiers and officials for decades.

He always denied the allegation, insisting he was only an above-board political leader. Few were convinced, but he did win election from Belfast to the British parliament – a seat he did not take up – and from the Republic of Ireland for its parliament in Dublin.

When republicans and unionists in Northern Ireland decided to put aside their differences and share power under the 1998 Good Friday Agreement, they had to overlook Adams's past to get him and his supporters on board.

The Nobel Peace Prize for 1998 was awarded to Catholic leader John Hume and Protestant leader David Trimble. Despite his crucial support for the agreement, Adams was too controversial to be named as the third winner.

21 March 2019

Terrorism and terrorist methods

Terrorists' beliefs and methods vary ...

But the consequences for the innocents are the same

What is terrorism?

Terrorist groups use violence and threats of violence to publicise their causes and as a means to achieve their goals. They often aim to influence or exert pressure on governments and government policies but reject democratic processes, or even democracy itself.

International terrorism

International terrorism from groups such as the Islamic State in Iraq and the Levant (ISIL) and Al Qaida present a threat for many others. They hold territory in places without functioning governments, making it easier for them to train recruits and plan complex, sophisticated attacks. Drawing on extreme interpretations of Islam to justify their actions, these groups often have the desire and capability to direct terrorist attacks against the West, and to inspire those already living there to carry out attacks of their own.

Northern Ireland-related terrorism

Northern Ireland-related terrorism continues to pose a serious threat to British interests. Although the Provisional Irish Republican Army (PIRA) has ceased its terrorist campaign and is now committed to the political process, some dissident republican groups continue to mount terrorist attacks, primarily against the security forces.

Domestic extremism

Domestic extremism mainly refers to individuals or groups that carry out criminal acts in pursuit of a larger agenda,

such as "right-wing extremists". They may seek to change legislation or influence domestic policy and try to achieve this outside of the normal democratic process.

Countering terrorism

MI5 has countered terrorist threats to UK interests, both at home and overseas, since the 1960s and the threat has developed significantly since then. It's challenging to understand the intentions and activities of secretive and sometimes highly organised groups. New and changing technologies make it increasingly difficult to obtain information necessary to disrupt the attack planning of these groups. Many are based in inaccessible areas overseas and there are limits to what can be done to prevent attacks planned and launched from abroad. Our techniques and the way we with work with other agencies both at home and abroad have to keep pace with the terrorists' capabilities.

Terrorists can use many different methods of attack. As well as using tried and tested methods, they are able to innovate, as demonstrated by the attacks on New York on 11 September 2001. More recently in Paris, we have seen a complex plot involving multiple attackers and various weapons, all coordinated to occur simultaneously.

Explosive devices

These can be delivered to their targets in vehicles, by post or by a person.

An explosive device within a vehicle is a common means of attack for some terrorist groups. Car bombs were frequently used by the IRA during the Troubles in Northern Ireland. International terrorist groups such as Al Qaida and the Islamic State of Iraq and the Levant (ISIL) often use suicide operatives in vehicles to improve the likelihood of the explosives detonating at the required moment.

Suicide bombers also carry an explosive device into the vicinity of a target individual or location. In Ankara in October 2015, for example, two people detonated suicide belts killing 102 people and injuring more than 500 others.

In December 2001, Richard Reid was thwarted in his attempt to bring down an airliner with a small improvised explosive device concealed in his shoes. In October 2015, a Metrojet flight from Sharm el-Sheikh to St Petersburg broke apart in the air, killing 224 people. The Sinai branch of ISIL claimed responsibility for the incident and ISIL later published photographs of the bomb that it alleged had been used.

Dissident republican groups in Northern Ireland continue to use a range of explosive devices. In 2011, an under-vehicle device was responsible for the death of Constable Ronan Kerr in Omagh, and several other such devices have been deployed since. Pipe bombs and radio-controlled, victim-operated and postal explosive devices have also been used in Northern Ireland recently.

Shootings and close quarter attacks

Terrorist groups have orchestrated a number of shootings and close quarter attacks targeting Westerners, in the Middle East, North Africa and Europe.

In June 2015, ISIL claimed responsibility for an attack on the Port El-Kantaoui tourist resort in Sousse, Tunisia. 38 people were killed, most of whom were tourists, including 30 British nationals.

In January 2015, brothers Said and Cherif Kouachi entered the Paris office of satirical newspaper *Charlie Hebdo* armed with assault weapons, killing 12 people and wounding many more. They claimed the attack on behalf of Al Qaida in the Arabian Peninsula (AQAP). A day later, a friend of the Kouachi brothers, Amedy Coulibaly, shot and killed an unarmed police officer. The following day he entered a kosher supermarket and killed four more people. Coulibaly claimed the attacks on behalf of ISIL.

In September 2014, ISIL released a speech calling for lone actor attacks against the West. This provided sanction for those inspired by ISIL to conduct attacks without any further reference to the group, stating that it's not necessary to travel to Syria to join ISIL: individuals can carry out attacks on the group's behalf and be recognised as a member. On 14 February, Omar Abdel El-Hussein attacked a freedom of speech debate at the Krudttonden cafe in Copenhagen, killing one attendee and injuring three police officers. Later the same day, he killed a security guard and injured two more police officers at the Great Synagogue. El-Hussein indicated that his actions were inspired by ISIL.

In November 2015, a terrorist cell conducted a series of coordinated attacks in Paris, using firearms and suicide bombs. The attackers targeted the Bataclan Theatre, the Stade de France and a number of cafes and restaurants, killing 130 people and injuring 368 more. ISIL claimed responsibility for the attacks the following day. This was the most sophisticated Western attack carried out by ISIL, involving at least nine operatives and using multiple weapons including automatic firearms and person-borne improvised explosive devices (PBIEDs).

Kidnappings

Islamist groups in conflict zones around the world actively seek to kidnap Western nationals for financial and propaganda gain. In the latter half of 2014, ISIL released videos claiming to show the murders of, amongst others, UK nationals David Haines and Alan Henning. Through these, ISIL hoped to spread fear and attempted to show its strength over the West. As well as in Syria and Iraq, the kidnap threat persists in Yemen and parts of West, North and East Africa where Islamist groups are active.

Surface to air missiles

An unsuccessful surface-to-air missile attack was attempted on an Israeli charter plane departing from Mombasa, Kenya, in November 2002, using a shoulder-launched Man-Portable Air Defence System (MANPADS). Similar attacks have been carried out against coalition aircraft in Iraq.

Chemical, biological and radiological (CBR) devices

To date, no such attacks have taken place in the UK. Alternative methods of attack, such as explosive devices, are more reliable, safer and easier for terrorists to acquire or use. Nevertheless, it is possible that Al Qaida, ISIL or other terrorist groups may seek to use chemical, biological or radiological material against the West.

In April 2005, Kamel Bourgass, an Algerian with known links to Al Qaida, was convicted of plotting to manufacture and spread poisons, including ricin, in the UK. Bourgass was sentenced to life in prison for the plot, and for fatally stabbing a police officer during his arrest.

Other methods of attack

In addition to physical attack methods, terrorists may also try to access information that may be of use to them. For example, they may try to radicalise an individual within an organisation who can provide "inside" information that helps to plan an attack.

2019

European Union Terrorism Situation and Trend Report 2018

An extract.

Trends

#1 In recent years there has been an increase in the frequency of jihadist attacks, but a decrease in the sophistication of their preparation and execution. Jihadist attacks, however, cause more deaths and casualties than any other terrorist attacks.

#2 Recent attacks by jihadist terrorists have followed three patterns: indiscriminate killings (London, March and June 2017; and Barcelona, August 2017); attacks on symbols of Western lifestyle (Manchester, May 2017); and attacks on symbols of authority (Paris, February, June and August 2017). New attacks in the EU by jihadist terrorists following one of these patterns or a combination thereof are highly likely.

#3 Jihadist attacks are committed primarily by homegrown terrorists, radicalised in their country of residence without having travelled to join a terrorist group abroad. This group of home-grown actors is highly diverse, consisting of individuals who have been born in the EU or have lived in the EU most of their lives, may have been known to the police but not for terrorist activities and often do not have direct links to the Islamic State (IS) or any other jihadist organisation.

#4 Recent attacks prove jihadist terrorists' preference for attacking people rather than other targets provoking less of an emotional response from the general public, such as damage to premises or loss of capital.

#5 Jihadist terrorists may operate in groups, but have often been found to be lone actors. They may have managed to keep their environment completely in the dark about their intentions prior to the attack. However, they may have friends and relatives in their environment who know of, sympathise with, facilitate or even assist in the preparation of an attack.

#6 The number of individuals travelling to the conflict zones in Iraq or Syria to join jihadist terrorist groups as foreign terrorist fighters has dropped significantly since 2015. The number of returnees was low in 2017.

#7 Online propaganda and networking via social media are still essential to terrorist attempts to reach out to EU audiences for recruitment, radicalisation and fundraising. As IS's capacities to produce new propaganda material are severely affected by losses of both operatives and infrastructure, the group continues to spread its message to wide audiences, by increasingly redistributing older material by new means.

#8 The often rudimentary and fragmented knowledge of Islam of (aspiring) jihadist terrorists makes them vulnerable to being influenced and manipulated by those who selectively use religious texts to fit a violent ideology.

#9 The degradation of IS organisational structures may reduce the attractiveness of the group. However, this may not affect the threat of jihadist terrorism, as disaffected IS members and sympathisers – including those residing in EU Member States – will likely continue to adhere to jihadist beliefs and might be drawn to join other groups, such as al-Qaeda. Al-Qaeda is still a powerful player and actively encourages terrorist attacks in the EU. Near-future terrorist activities in the EU ordered, guided or inspired by al-Qaeda or other jihadist organisations remain a realistic possibility.

#10 Ethno-nationalist and separatist terrorist attacks continue to far outnumber attacks carried out by violent extremists inspired by any other ideologies or motivations.

#11 The violent right-wing extremist spectrum is expanding, partly fuelled by fears of a perceived Islamisation of society and anxiety over migration.

#12 There is no evidence of chemical, biological, radiological or nuclear (CBRN) weaponry being used by terrorists in the EU, despite indications of jihadist terrorists taking an active interest in its possibilities. Improvised explosive devices, firearms and improvised weapon, such as knives and vehicles, are the weapons of choice with which recent attacks were carried out. These weapons, except for explosive devices, do not require much preparation or special skills to be employed in terrorist attacks, which are either carefully prepared or carried out spontaneously.

Types of terrorism

The TE-SAT categorises terrorist organisations by their source of motivation. However, many groups have a mixture of motivating ideologies, although usually one ideology or motivation dominates. It is worth noting that a categorisation of individuals and terrorist groups based on the ideology or goals they espouse should not be confused with motivating factors and the paths to radicalisation. The underlying causes that lead people to radicalisation and terrorism must be sought in the surroundings (structural factors) and personal interpretations (psychological factors) of the individual. The choice of categories used in the TE-SAT reflects the current situation in the EU, as reported by Member States. The categories are not necessarily mutually exclusive.

Jihadist

Jihadist terrorist acts are those that are committed out of a mind-set that rejects democracy on religious grounds and uses the historical comparison with the crusades of the Middle Ages to describe current situations, in which it is believed that Sunni Islam is facing a crusader alliance composed of Shi'is, Christians and Jews.

Right-wing

Right-wing terrorist organisations seek to change the entire political, social and economic system on an extremist right-wing model. A core concept in right-wing extremism is supremacism, or the idea that a certain group of people sharing a common element (nation, race, culture, etc.) is superior to all other people. Seeing themselves in a supreme position, the particular group considers it is their natural right to rule over the rest of the population. Racist behaviour, authoritarianism, xenophobia and hostility to immigration are commonly-found attitudes in right-wing extremists. Right-wing terrorism refers to the use of terrorist violence right-wing groups. Variants of right-wing extremist groups are the neo-Nazi, neo-fascist and ultra-nationalist formations.

Left-wing and anarchist terrorism

Left-wing terrorist groups seek to replace the entire political, social and economic system of a state by introducing a communist or socialist structure and a classless society. Their ideology is often Marxist-Leninist. A sub-category of left-wing extremism is anarchist terrorism which promotes a revolutionary, anti-capitalist and anti-authoritarian agenda. Examples of left-wing terrorist groups are the Italian Brigate Rosse (Red Brigades) and the Greek Revolutionary Organisation 17 November.

Ethno-nationalism and separatism

Ethno-nationalist and separatist terrorist groups are motivated by nationalism, ethnicity and/or religion. Separatist groups seek to carve out a state for themselves from a larger country, or annex a territory from one country to that of another. Left- or right-wing ideological elements are not uncommon in these types of groups. The Irish Republican Army (IRA), the Basque ETA, and the Kurdish PKK organisations fall into this category.

Single issue

Single-issue extremist groups aim to change a specific policy or practice, as opposed to replacing the whole political, social, and economic system in a society. The groups within this category are usually concerned with animal rights, environmental protection, anti-abortion campaigns, etc. Examples of groups in this category are the Earth Liberation Front (ELF), and the Animal Liberation Front (ALF).

2018

Terrorism in Britain: a brief history

An article from **The Conversation.**

THE CONVERSATION

By Joseph McQuade PHD candidate and Gates Scholar, University of Cambridge

The attack on Mancester Arena is the deadliest on British soil since the July 7 bombings of 2005, in which four suicide bombers killed 52 people in central London.

It is also the latest event in a long history of terrorism in Britain. And it is a history that transcends the narrow political and religious dimensions often associated with it today.

It is almost impossible to pinpoint the very first act of terrorism carried out within British territory. The most famous incident in early modern history is probably the gunpowder plot of 1605 when Guy Fawkes attempted to blow up the House of Lords. And although he is the best remembered (on 5th November), Fawkes did not act alone. He was part of a larger network of 13 conspirators who sought to destroy parliament and trigger a popular uprising.

In the second half of the 19th century, European anarchism introduced the idea of "propaganda by deed" as a tactic of anti-government resistance. This consisted of the assassination of government officials and bomb attacks in public places such as cafes and theatres.

Although anarchist attacks were actually more common in continental Europe, England was an important hub for anarchist thought. The less-restrictive laws of the United Kingdom made it a haven for radicals fleeing political repression in their own countries.

In the same period, the heavy death toll of the Great Famine in Ireland from 1846 to 1852 prompted calls for Irish home rule and resulted in the formation of networks of radical revolutionaries, the Fenians.

Although the largest Fenian campaigns were waged in Canada and in Ireland itself, attacks within England included the bombing of Clerkenwell Prison in London in 1867, in which 12 people were killed and more than 100 injured. The result was a severe backlash by British authorities and the public, which undermined the political reforms that would have made future attacks less likely.

In 1909, the Indian revolutionary Madan Lal Dhingra assassinated a British official on the steps of the Imperial Institute in London. This followed a number of assassinations and bombings in India, as militant networks of anti-colonial radicals attempted to destabilise British imperial rule by initiating a "reign of terror".

Dhingra was apprehended and executed, but his brazen attack in the middle of London provoked panic within metropolitan Britain. It also resulted in increasingly intrusive surveillance of Indian students in London. This in turn fuelled the fire of Indian nationalism, most famously manifested in Gandhi's non-violent independence movement.

Made in Britain

A nation scarred

More recently, the IRA conducted a sustained insurgency against the British government from the early 1970s to the late 1990s. The bulk of the violence took place within the political and religious tensions of Northern Ireland. Belfast looked like a war zone, with hundreds of lethal attacks carried out by both the IRA and pro-British groups. The IRA also carried out acts of terror in England, including a truck bombing in Manchester in June 1996 that injured 220 people and caused some £700 million of damage.

Terrorism, by definition, seeks to spread terror. It might be tempting to consider the early 21st century as a period of unparalleled and incomprehensible acts of senseless violence. But it is not. Sadly these kinds of acts are not new.

This does not mean we should resign ourselves to living in perpetual dread as we await the next attack, whether it's in Britain, France, Russia, Australia, Egypt or America. Nor that we should exacerbate the situation by lashing out against those who may make easy targets for retaliatory anger. But as we try to process the grief and rage that are natural reactions to the attack in Manchester, reflecting on the lessons of the past may be the surest route towards building a more peaceful future.

25 May 2017

Terrorism in Great Britain: the statistics

A table from the House of Commons library briefing paper – number CBP7613.

By Grahame Allen and Noel Dempsey

The majority of people arrested for terrorism related offences in Great Britain since 11 September 2001 have been British nationals: 58% of people declared they were a British national at the time of their arrest.

On an annual basis the proportion of those arrested for terrorism offences who are British nationals has increased.

In 2001/02 29% were British nationals. In 2016/17 72% of those arrested were British nationals. In the year ending 31 December 2017, 67% of all those arrested were British nationals. The chart below shows the increase in the proportion of British nationals arrested.

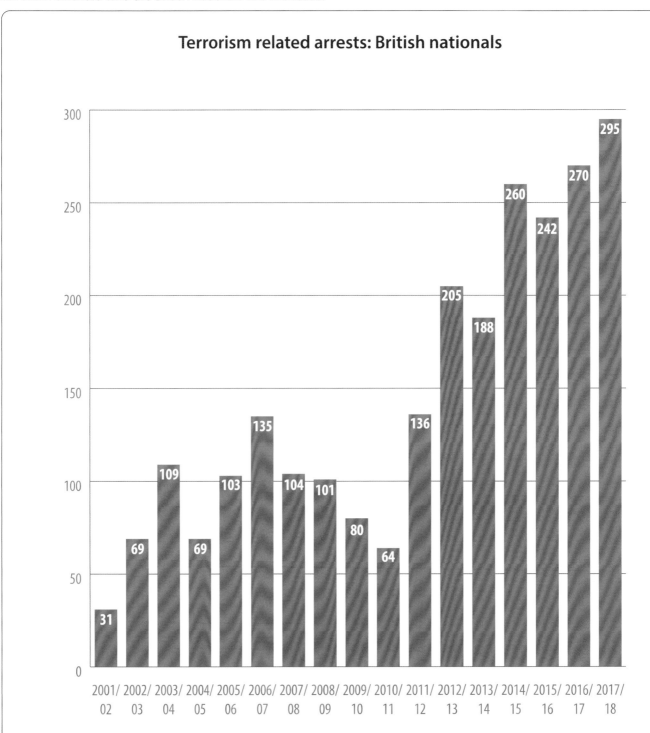

Terrorism related arrests: British nationals

Year	Value
2001/02	31
2002/03	69
2003/04	109
2004/05	69
2005/06	103
2006/07	135
2007/08	104
2008/09	101
2009/10	80
2010/11	64
2011/12	136
2012/13	205
2013/14	188
2014/15	260
2015/16	242
2016/17	270
2017/18	295

Note: Data for 2001/02 is for 11 September 2001 onwards

Source: Home Office, Operation of Police powers under the Terrorism Act 2000 and subsequent legislation: quarterly update to March 2018, table QA.12a

Terrorism related arrests: top 30 nationalities

Nationality	Arrests	Nationality	Arrests
British	2,219	Albania	21
Algeria	173	Portugal	21
Pakistan	158	Netherlands	20
Iraq	146	Syria	20
Afghanistan	85	Palestine	19
Iran	81	Germany	18
Turkey	69	Sudan	17
Somalia	66	Ethiopia	17
India	60	Saudi Arabia	17
Ireland	45	Romania	16
Libya	42	Poland	16
Bangladesh	38	Lebanon	16
Sri Lanka	34	Jordan	15
France	32	Italy	14
Morocco	24	Spain	13

Source: Source: Home Office, Operation of Police powers under the Terrorism Act 2000 and subsequent legislation: quarterly update to December 2017, table QA.12a

Since 11 September 2001 there have been 100 different nationalities arrested for terrorism related offences. The table above shows the top 30 nationalities of people arrested.

After Great Britain, the next ten most common nationalities (Algeria through to Libya) account for 24% of all terrorism related arrests (925) – this is greater than the next 89 nationalities combined (17%).

7 June 2018

www.parliament.uk

Operation of police powers under the Terrorism Act 2000: quarterly update to December 2018

An extract from the Home Office statistical bulletin.

Key findings

Arrests and outcomes

There were 273 arrests for terrorism-related activity in the year ending 31 December 2018, a decrease of 41% compared with the 465 arrests in the previous year. The fall is partly due to a relatively large number of arrests in the previous reporting year in the wake of terrorist attacks in London and Manchester.

Of the 273 arrests for terrorism-related activity:

◆ 102 (37%) resulted in a charge, of which 81 were charged with terrorism-related offences

◆ 99 people arrested (36%) were released without charge

◆ 23 (8%) persons were released on bail pending further investigation

◆ 17 (6%) faced alternative action

◆ 32 (12%) cases were pending at the time of data provision.

Of the 81 persons charged with a terrorism-related offence, 38 had been prosecuted, all of whom had been convicted. A total of 38 people were awaiting prosecution, three were not proceeded against and two received other outcomes.

Falls in the number of arrests were seen across all ethnic groups. The rate of reduction in the number of Asians arrested was highest of all ethnic groups. This resulted in the proportion of all arrestees who were Asian (32%) being lower than those who were White (43%). The proportion of White people arrested exceeded the proportion of Asian people arrested.

Court proceedings

Court proceedings in the year ending 31 December 2018 will include a number of persons arrested and charged in a previous year. A total of 84 persons were tried following charges brought by the Crown Prosecution Service Counter Terrorism Division (CPS CTD) for terrorism-related offences. This was a fall of two on the 86 persons tried in the previous year. Of the 84 persons proceeded against, 76 were convicted. In the remaining eight cases the defendant was found not guilty.

Terrorist prisoners

As at 31 December 2018, there were 221 persons in custody in Great Britain for terrorism-related offences, a decrease of 1% on the 224 persons in the previous year. This was the first fall in the number of persons in custody since the year ending December 2013, and follows an upward trend seen between 2013 and 2017.

Of those in custody, the majority (79%) were categorised as holding Islamist-extremist views, a further 13% as holding far right-wing ideologies and 8% other ideologies.

Of those in custody:

◆ 186 (84%) had been convicted

◆ 35 (16%) were being held on remand (held in custody until a later date when a trial or a sentencing hearing will take place).

Use of other police powers

In the year ending 31 December 2018:

◆ the Metropolitan Police Service (MPS) carried out 610 stop and searches under section 43 of the Terrorism Act (TACT) 2000, a fall of 20% when compared with the previous year

◆ there were 55 resultant arrests giving an arrest rate of 9%, up one percentage point on the previous year

◆ there were 11,891 physical examinations of suspects under Schedule 7 of TACT 2000 in Great Britain, a decrease of 27% from the previous year (16,349), continuing the downward trend seen in recent years

Demographics of persons arrested

This section provides more detail on the demographic and other characteristics of persons arrested. It includes data on:

◆ sex

◆ age

◆ ethnic appearance

◆ nationality

◆ category of terrorist (for example international terrorism, domestic terrorism or Northern Ireland relate terrorism).

Sex

As in previous years, and similar to other types of crime, the vast majority of those arrested for terrorism-related activity were males. However, 31 of the 273 arrests were females (11%), a fall of 32 on the previous year's total of 63 females arrested. This was the lowest number of females arrested since the year ending December 2013. Despite the fall, the total number of females arrested was above the average arrested per year (24) since the data collection began. The proportion of females arrested was above the series average (9%) in each of the past six years.

Arrests and outcomes

Proportion of persons arrested for terrorist-related activity by ethnic appearance [1,2], year ending 31 December 2017 and 31 December 2018, compared with total proportions since 11 September 2001

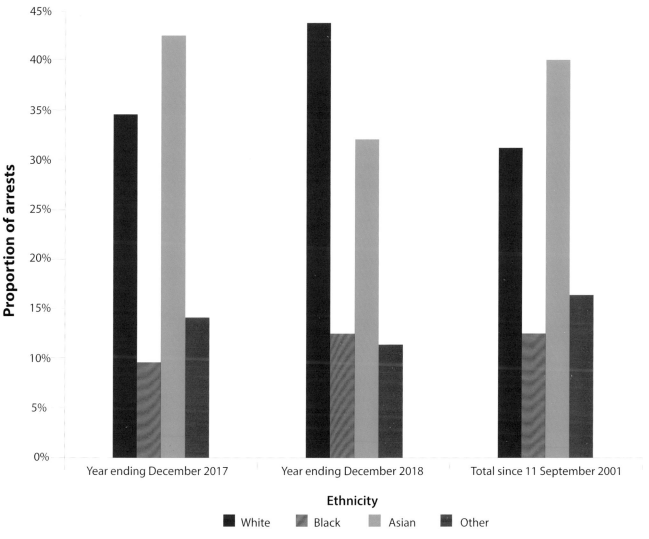

Source: *NCTPOC*

Notes: 1. As recorded by the police at time of arrest.   2. Excludes those whose ethnicity is not known

Age

There were falls in the number of arrests across all age-groups compared with the previous year. As in previous years, the '30 and over' age group accounted for the most arrests (48%). Those aged under 18 accounted for 6% of arrests, a similar level to the previous year, which was the highest proportion of under 18s arrested since the data collection began in 2001.

Ethnic appearance as recorded by the arresting officer

There were falls in the number of arrests across all ethnic groups. The largest decrease was seen for those of Asian ethnic appearance, which decreased by 56% when compared with the previous year (from 196 arrests to 86 arrests). Whilst there was also a 26% decrease in the number of arrests of White people (from 160 arrests to 118); this was the third highest number of arrests of White people in a calendar year since the data collection began in 2001.

Arrests of persons of White ethnic appearance accounted for 43% of arrests, an increase of nine percentage points on the previous year. In contrast, those of Asian ethnic appearance accounted for 32% of terrorist-related arrests, down 11 percentage points on the previous year. The proportion of White people arrested now exceeds the proportion of Asian people arrested. The proportion of those arrested who were of Black ethnic appearance increased by three percentage points to account for 13% of all arrests. Those of 'Other' ethnic appearance accounted for 12% of arrests, down two percentage points on the previous year.

7 March 2019

What is the Terrorism Act 2000?

By India Wentworth

This Act is the permanent anti-terrorism legislation in the UK. It works to combat the global problem of terrorism and the ways that terrorism is funded. With 2017 being arguably one of the most challenging years for police and security due to the UK terror attacks, the fight on terror is far from over. MI5's Andrew Parker stresses the severity of the problem by highlighting that the tempo of country terrorism operations is the highest he has ever seen it in his 34-year career.

In many cases, terrorist operations are fuelled from legitimate sources of money. By using clean money for deadly causes, they are tainting it, hence the name reverse money laundering.

The Act can be seen as a way to combat the financing of terrorism and consequently reduce the number of successful terrorist operations by leaving people more aware of where their money is going and therefore cuts off the money source for many terrorist groups.

Contents of the Act

- Replaces temporary legislation first passed in the 1970s to combat terrorism. The Prevention of Terrorism Act 1989, the Northern Ireland Act 1996, and parts of the Criminal Justice Act 1998 were all replaced with the Terrorism Act 2000.

- Widens the definition of "terrorism" to apply to domestic matters as well as international incidents, therefore having the authority to cover more situations.

- Expands the definition of terrorism so that it refers to action that is used (or threatened) for the purpose of advancing a "political, religious or ideological cause" rather than just "violence for political ends". They define "action" as including: violence against a person, damage to property, serious risk to the health or safety of others and behaviour designed to interfere with or disrupt an electronic system. All authorities work off this definition to create a consistency across the board.

- Allows the police to hold people arrested for terrorism offences for a period of seven days.

- Gives the secretary of state the power to ban organisations and set out a range of offences connected with those organisations.

- Develops offences that are associated with financing and support for terrorism, as well as criminalising specific offences such as possessing information for terrorism or inciting overseas terrorism.

- Grants the police the authority to stop and search a person/vehicle without suspicion if they're operating in a designated area.

Evolution of the Act

The IRA ceasefire in 1994 was the event that triggered anti-terrorism action. The hopes for peace were raised for the nation after the deaths of more than 3,000 people caused the government to accept that there was a need for permanent terrorism legislation.

Lord Lloyd of Berwick was leading the inquiries for the government at the time, and he was the man that pushed for the changes. He wanted the Prevention of Terrorism Act to be reformed because of the fact it was always temporary provisions.

The definition of terrorism soon went on to include the term "violence". A move that proved to be controversial, especially when it widened even further, stating that terrorism included the use of "serious violence against persons or property". This was because critics claimed that this change would essentially put people who dig up genetically modified crops in the same category as an IRA bomber and could therefore be used to tamper with legitimate protests.

Many MPs expressed discomfort about the possible impact of the permanent legislation. This was because they feared the law gave the government permanent powers to restrain political protest. Additionally, they were concerned by the decision that allowed the Home Secretary to outlaw organisations believed to be involved in terrorism.

Specifically, section 44 has received heavy criticism from protesters who claim the police have used the power to prevent peaceful protests. Despite the House of Lords rejecting these claims, the use and misuse of stop and search remains controversial as part of the Act. When Walter Wolfgang was forcibly removed from the audience of a political speech, police used their powers to prevent him from returning to the conference.

Since then, this section of the Act has been reformed and now police have to "reasonably suspect" a person in order to stop and search them. However, the area still leaves people split, with some arguing it makes the lives of the police harder, whilst the human rights campaigners 'Liberty' stress that the power had "criminalised and alienated more people than it ever protected".

6 September 2018

www.delta-net.com

Terrorism in the EU: terror attacks, deaths and arrests

In recent years there has been an increase in terrorist threats and attacks, beginning in 2015 with the killings at the *Charlie Hebdo* magazine office in Paris.

Terrorist attacks in numbers

In 2017, 62 people were killed in 33 religiously-inspired terrorist attacks in the EU, compared to 135 deaths in 13 attacks in 2016, according to Europol figures. In both years ten attacks were considered as "completed" by national governments, because they achieved their target. In 2017 many more attacks were foiled or failed compared to 2016: 23 in 2017 compared to three the year before.

In 2015, the number of deaths caused by this kind of attack reached a peak of 150, sharply up from four in 2014. In 2017, the attacks were much less lethal.

Presenting the EU's terrorism situation and trend report 2018 to Parliament's civil liberties committee on 20 June, Manuel Navarrete, head of Europol's European Counter Terrorism Centre, said, "The attacks are less sophisticated, there are more, but fortunately they produce less victims."

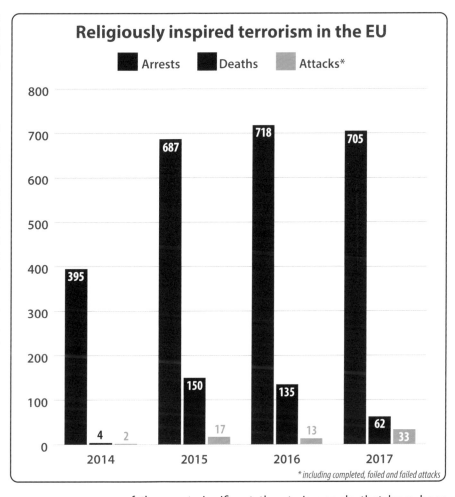

Religiously inspired terrorism in the EU

Arrests ■ Deaths ■ Attacks* ▨

* including completed, foiled and failed attacks

Situation in 2017

Ten of the 33 attacks were assessed as "completed" in 2017, while 12 failed to reach their objectives in full and 11 were foiled, mostly in France and the UK.

That year 62 people died: UK (35), Spain (16), Sweden (5), France (3), Finland (2) and Germany (1). A further 819 people were injured.

A total of 705 people were arrested in 18 EU countries (373 in France) on suspicion of involvement in jihadist terrorist activities.

EU cooperation

The reinforced cooperation between EU countries, sharing information, has helped to prevent attacks, stop them or limit their impact, according to Navarrete. "The plots are identified earlier because the tools for intelligence and police are used in a more accurate way." He added: "We are preventing [attacks] and mitigating the number of people that are killed or injured.".

Potential threats

However, despite the success of the common approach, it remains important to stay vigilant. Navarrete said: "One of the most significant threats is people that have been arrested for their connection with the foreign fighter phenomenon and will be released shortly."

Most attacks are now perpetrated by home-grown terrorist radicalised in the European country where they are living, without having necessarily travelled to conflict zones such as Syria or Iraq, he said.

"There are still people returning from conflict zones like Iraq, but the figures were very low in 2017."

No systematic use of migration routes by terrorists

Some people have been concerned about the risk posed by migrants trying to enter Europe. Navarrette said: 'We haven´t seen a systematic use of these routes by terrorists.' However, he added that Europol had identified "some terrorists" who try to use migration routes to enter the EU and that is why it has reinforced its cooperation with countries such as Greece and Italy and remains "vigilant".

25 July 2018

Terrorist groups

An extract from the **Global Terrorism Index 2018.**

etermining which terrorist groups are the most active and responsible for the most deaths can be difficult, as many groups have regional affiliates and other groups working in partnership or partially under the same command. For the purposes of this section, IEP does not include affiliates in its definition of a terrorist group. For example ISIL refers only to the Islamic State of Iraq and the Levant, and does not include the Khorasan chapter or Sinai Province of the Islamic State, despite the strong connections between the two groups. Similarly, Al-Shabaab is counted as a single group, rather than an affiliate of Al-Qa'ida.

The four terrorist groups responsible for the most deaths in 2017 were the Islamic State of Iraq and the Levant (ISIL), the Taliban, Al-Shabaab and Boko Haram. These four groups were responsible for 10,632 deaths from terrorism, representing 56.5% of total deaths in 2017. In 2012, just prior to the large increase in terrorist activity around the world, these four groups were responsible for 32% of all deaths from terrorism. A decade ago, they accounted for just six per cent.

The past decade has experienced the largest surge in terrorist activity in the past fifty years. These four groups are responsible for 44% of the deaths in the decade. However, all of the groups other than Al-Shabaab have experienced falls in terrorist activity in the past few years.

Islamic State of Iraq & the Levant (ISIL)

The Islamic State of Iraq and the Levant, often referred to as ISIL, ISIS or Daesh, was the most active terrorist organisation in 2017, a position it has held since 2015. Primarily active in Iraq and Syria – the countries in which it sought to create a caliphate, or autonomous Islamist state, ISIL's presence and impact decreased substantially in these countries in 2017.

Changes since 2016

ISIL-related deaths are at their lowest point since 2013. ISIL suffered severe losses in 2017, leading to a reduction in the number of attacks carried out by the group. International coalitions, Syrian and Iraqi rebel forces successfully reclaimed the cities of Mosul and Raqqa, two of ISIL's strongholds and claims to territorial legitimacy. Having lost 60% of its territory and 80% of its revenue since 2015, ISIL's capacity to create a caliphate has diminished greatly. The turn-around in its fortunes is remarkable as 2016 was its deadliest year on record.

Deaths committed by the group decreased from 9,150 to 4,350 in 2017, a decline of 52%. Injuries which they inflicted in their terrorist attacks fell similarly by a margin of 57%, and the number of attacks fell by 22%. The lethality of ISIL attacks, or deaths per attack, also dropped from eight to 4.9 deaths per attack.

Despite its decline, ISIL is still active in ten countries in 2017, highlighting the spread of their operations. ISIL committed attacks in 286 cities around the world in four different regions: Asia-Pacific, Europe, MENA and the Russia and Eurasia region. Of all ISIL attacks, 98% of incidents and 98% of deaths occurred within the MENA region. 90% of all terror attacks and 81% of terror-related deaths from ISIL occurred in Iraq alone. Deaths from ISIL attacks in Europe decreased by 6%, from 198 in 2016 to 64 in 2017.

In 2017, 1,524 deaths and 254 attacks confirmed by ISIL occurred in the Iraqi city of Mosul, compared to 1,851 deaths in Mosul in 2016. The four deadliest attacks committed by ISIL were all in the Iraqi province of Nineveh and resulted in a total of 693 deaths.

In MENA, terrorism deaths committed by ISIL also substantially decreased, falling from 8,930 in 2016 to 4,264, indicating a decline in the group's activity both in the Middle East and elsewhere. As its strength has dwindled in its Iraqi and Syrian strongholds, ISIL has looked to shift resources into other countries and regions. ISIL and its affiliates were active in 25 countries in 2017, up from 14 in 2014.

Despite territorial, financial, and logistical losses in 2017, ISIL's status as the world's deadliest terror group still poses a major threat through both its ideological profile around the world and numerous affiliate chapters based in neighbouring regions. For example, ISIL was responsible for 18 deaths in the Asia-Pacific region in 2017, all of which occurred in the Philippines.

Tactics favoured by ISIL

69% of attacks staged by the Islamic State were bombings or explosions, 80% of which resulted in at least one fatality. These attacks resulted in 2,387 fatalities in 2017. The next most common forms of attack were hostage takings and assassinations, which made up 12% of ISIL attacks in 2017, killing 988 people. In 2017, 479 attacks were targeted specifically towards private civilians, down from 663 attacks in 2016.

ISIL's attacks on military and police personnel became less deadly. Despite staging only ten fewer attacks in 2017 towards police and military personnel, these attacks resulted in 1,293 fewer deaths than the prior year, a 60% reduction. The weakened success rate of ISIL's attacks in 2017 is another sign that the group's capacity is declining.

Taliban

The Taliban emerged in Afghanistan in 1994 as a reactionary group that combined both mujahideen that had previously fought against the 1979 Soviet invasion, and groups of Pashtun tribesmen. The Taliban took control of Afghanistan in 1996. The group declared the country an Islamic emirate and promoted its leader to the role of head of state. Following the 2001 NATO invasion of Afghanistan, the Taliban was ousted, but it has since been steadily regaining control of its lost territory. As of mid-2017, it was estimated that the

Four deadliest terrorist groups in 2017 (1988-2017)

ISIL, The Taliban, and Boko Haram have all seen falls in terrorist activity over the past two years

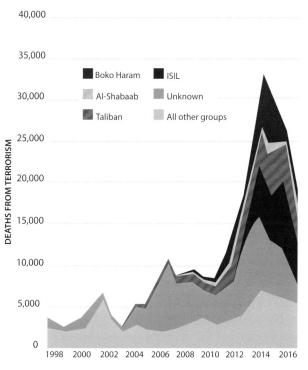

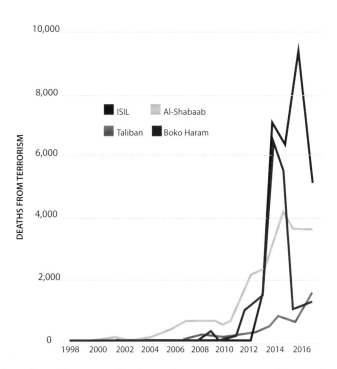

Taliban controlled over 11% of the country and contested another 29% of Afghanistan's 398 districts. However, these estimates are likely to be highly conservative. While the Taliban's activity is similar to the previous year, it maintains a highly active presence in over 70% of Afghani provinces. In recent months, the Taliban has appeared receptive to peace talks, however, the fighting has continued.

Changes since 2016

The number of deaths from terrorism caused by the Taliban remained steady in 2017. However, the years 2015 to 2017 have also seen much higher levels of terrorism committed by the Taliban than in the preceding decade. In total, 82% of deaths from terrorism committed by the Taliban since 2002 have occurred in the last five years.

Unlike ISIL, the Taliban is active solely in a single country. All of the 3,571 deaths and 699 terrorist attacks in 2017 occurred within Afghanistan. However, the Taliban's Pakistani affiliate group, Tehrik-i-Taliban Pakistan (TTP), was responsible for 233 deaths and 56 attacks in Pakistan in 2017, demonstrating a Taliban-related presence outside of Afghanistan. As a whole, terror attacks by the Taliban are becoming more deadly with attacks in 2016 killing an average of 4.2 persons per attack, rising to 5.1 persons in 2017.

The deadliest attack committed by the Taliban was from a suicide explosion in Gardez, Paktika, killing 74 people and injuring an additional 236 people. The majority of terrorism by the Taliban is committed in Afghanistan's southern provinces, but almost all districts in the country experienced attacks at some point in 2017.

Tactics favoured by the Taliban

In 2017, the Taliban switched focus from attacks on civilians, towards attacks on police and military personnel. The Taliban killed 2,419 police and military personnel in 2017, up

from the 1,782 deaths in the previous year. The number of attacks also increased from 369 to 386 in 2017.

The increased focus on the military was offset by a large reduction in civilian deaths with the Taliban being responsible for 548 civilian terrorism deaths in 2017 compared to 1,223 deaths in the prior year. Attacks on civilians also fell, dropping from 254 attacks in 2016 to 138 in 2017.

Armed assaults and bombings were the most common type of attack used by the Taliban, accounting for 54% of all attacks. Although the number of bombings decreased 18%, total deaths from bombings increased by 17%.

Al-Shabaab

Al-Shabaab, a Salafist militant group active in East Africa, first emerged in a battle over Somalia's capital in the summer of 2006. As an Al-Qa'ida affiliate terrorist group based in Somalia and Kenya, Al-Shabaab pursues Islamist statehood aspirations in Somalia.

In more recent years, Al-Shabaab has gained global recognition following many years of deadly attacks concentrated around the capital city of Mogadishu and attacks in the neighbouring states of Kenya, Ethiopia and Uganda. African Union peacekeeping forces known as AMISOM have been fighting Al-Shabaab since 2007 with the help of US and UN support. In 2017, the first wave of US troops and airstrikes were deployed in Somalia to fight against Al-Shabaab.

Changes since 2016

In 2017, Al-Shabaab overtook Boko Haram as the deadliest terror group in sub-Saharan Africa for the first time since 2010. The total number of deaths increased by 93% from 2016 to 2017. Of the 1,457 deaths committed by Al-Shabaab in 2017, 67% took place in the capital city of Mogadishu. The total number of terror incidents between 2016 and 2017 increased by only ten attacks, meaning the lethality of Al-Shabaab attacks in Somalia increased from 2.2 deaths per attack to 4.1 deaths per attack, mostly as the result of a single attack that killed 588 people. This was the deadliest terror attack globally in 2017.

Al-Shabaab activity in Somalia is scattered throughout the whole country. Although 67% of deaths occurred in the Banaadir region where Mogadishu is located, terrorist activity is scattered around the southern and eastern regions of Bari and Shebelle and the northern Puntland. To this day, Al-Shabaab holds significant organisational and territorial capacity against Somali and AMISOM forces.

On 14 October 2017, Al-Shabaab committed the deadliest terror attack of the year through a suicide and truck-bombing targeting a hotel and highway intersection in Mogadishu, killing 588 and injuring 316 individuals. This bombing was the world's deadliest terror attack since 2014 and the fifth-deadliest terror attack since the year 2000.

Terrorism deaths committed by Al-Shabaab in Kenya in 2017 also increased to 100. However, this is much lower than 2014, when the group killed 256 people. The deaths in 2017 occured in the Lamu, Garissa and Mandera counties. Half of deaths in Kenya during 2017 occurred in the Lamu County.

Tactics favoured by Al-Shabaab

The fragility of Somalia's political and security institutions has allowed Al-Shabaab to mount a number of highly-destructive terrorist attacks. Two of the twenty largest terrorist attacks of 2017 were carried out by Al-Shabaab and the group was able to carry out 17 successful attacks that killed ten or more people. The lethality of its bombing and explosive attacks was the highest of the four terrorist groups examined.

Al-Shabaab targeted many different groups in 2017, with the highest proportion of attacks directed at government targets followed by private citizens. However, Al-Shabaab's deadliest attacks were directed against business targets, including the suicide bombing which killed 588 people.

Boko Haram

Jama'tu Ahlis Sunna Lidda'awati wal-Jihad, more popularly known as Boko Haram, once the world's deadliest terror group, has experienced a significant decline since its peak in 2014. However, the group remains the most active terrorist organisation in Nigeria and until 2017 was the deadliest terror group in sub-Saharan Africa.

Originally formed in Northeast Nigeria bordering the Lake Chad region, the terror group has spread into Chad, Cameroon and Niger. Recently, internal tensions have led to multiple Boko Haram splinter groups forming. The largest splinter group is the Islamic State West African Province (ISWAP), which has claimed responsibility for a number of brutal attacks on midwives and aid workers in 2018. Both Boko Haram and ISWAP have sworn allegiance to the Islamic State.

'The Islamic State of Iraq and the Levant (ISIL), the Taliban, Al-Shabaab, and Boko Haram were responsible for 10,632 deaths from terrorism in 2017.'

Nigeria's counterterrorism response in combatting Boko Haram has been interrupted by the emergence of other extremist groups, most notably the Fulani extremists. The Fulani extremists have attacked civilians and military forces in the country. However, the sizeable drop in deaths and terror incidents since 2014 indicate the success of Nigeria's Civilian Join Task Force and international coalitions. Alongside its counterinsurgency plan, the Nigerian government also struggles with negotiations and reintegration efforts regarding its long-term strategy to deal with Boko Haram and its associates.

Changes since 2016

After a significant fall in activity between 2014 and 2016, Boko Haram increased its activity in 2017. It committed 40% more attacks and was responsible for 15% more deaths in 2017, carrying out 272 attacks and killing 1,254 people. Their attacks have been slightly less successful in 2017, with the average number of people killed per attack falling from 5.6 to 4.6. Deaths committed by the group have gone down substantially since the group's peak in 2014 when it killed 6,612 people, in part because of the intra-group dissolution weakening the group's capacity. Deaths committed are down 83.2% since their peak in 2014.

Of all the deaths committed by Boko Haram in 2017, 81% occurred in Nigeria, the remainder in Cameroon and Niger. This is up from 70% in 2016 and highlights the decreased reach of the organisation. 82% of deaths in Nigeria took place in the country's Borno State, and another 17% occurred in the Adamawa State. Boko Haram has concentrated its activity in the Lake Chad region in the past year.

Of the ten deadliest attacks Boko Haram committed in 2017, all were in Nigeria and nine were in the Borno State. The group's deadliest attack was an armed assault against a Frontier Exploration Services convoy that killed 69 people, most of whom were civilians.

Tactics Favoured by Boko Haram

Boko Haram has specialised in maximum-impact bombings and explosions since its initial insurgency in 2009.9 It is well known for its use of more uncommon terrorist tactics, including mass hostage takings and the extensive use of children and women as suicide bombers. Nearly four in five bombings in 2016 were suicide bombings with one in five committed by women.

November 2018

Right-wing extremist violence is our biggest threat. The numbers don't lie.

By Jonathan Greenblatt, National Director of the Anti-Defamation League

Every year, extremism takes a deadly toll around the world. No region is immune – not the Middle East, not Europe, and not the United States. In 2018, there were at least 50 Americans killed by extremists from different movements.

Many of the victims were Jews. Eleven members of the Tree of Life synagogue in Pittsburgh lost their lives in October at the hands of a vicious white supremacist convinced that Jews were engineering mass immigration of non-whites into the US. Blaze Bernstein, a young gay Jewish man, was murdered in California last January by a former classmate who allegedly was a member of a violent neo-Nazi group. And five of the 17 victims of Parkland school shooter Nikolas Cruz, a budding white supremacist, were Jewish.

But Jews were hardly the only victims of deadly extremist violence in 2018.

A white supremacist at a Veterans Affairs home in Tennessee allegedly set his African-American roommate on fire, then boasted about it to a white supremacist group.

Just months before the Tree of Life shooting, another Pittsburgh white supremacist was charged with stabbing an African-American man to death while on a quest to visit bars and repeat the "n-word" until being kicked out. In November, Scott Beierle opened fire at a Florida yoga studio, killing two and wounding four others in an apparent spree of misogynistic violence.

In 17 different incidents across the country last year, people lost their lives to extremists. Some attacks were ideological in nature, others personal; for a few, the motivation remains murky. The 50 deaths topped the 37 individuals killed by extremists in 2017 and made 2018 the fourth-deadliest year on record for domestic extremist-related killings since 1970.

Largely absent from this list of killers were extremists motivated by radical interpretations of Islam. Only one of the 50 murderers had any connection to Islamist extremism – and even he had ties to white supremacy. In 2018, the US. was thankfully spared the mass murders by Islamist extremists we've seen in recent years.

To be clear, there were Islamist-inspired terrorist plots and people arrested on charges such as providing support to such individuals. And we have seen real challenges from this type of violence abroad. However, it is a reminder about the unfairness of peddling anti-Muslim bias or making hysterical claims about faith-based extremists grounded in fiction rather than fact.

And yet these statistics communicate a clear message that the U.S. must pay more attention to dangers posed by domestic right-wing extremism – without neglecting the genuine need to prevent all forms of extremist violence. There are more than a dozen active right-wing extremist movements in the US. that are violent, such as white supremacists, anti-government sovereign citizens and militias, and anti-Muslim and anti-immigrant extremists.

The fact is right-wing extremists collectively have been responsible for more than 70 percent of the 427 extremist-related killings over the past 10 years, far outnumbering those committed by left-wing extremists or domestic Islamist extremists – even with the sharp rise of Islamist-extremist killings in the past five years.

These murder statistics send us a clear message: right-wing extremist violence needs to be addressed. It will not go away on its own. Indeed, as our Center on Extremism has documented, the white supremacist movement is growing. The Pittsburgh synagogue shooting in October was a reminder of what can happen when anti-Semitism, a key ingredient of white supremacist bile, is left unchecked. If we want a safe society for Jews and all Americans, we must address this problem.

Extremist, right-wing violence is a problem that can be addressed. Congress should ensure that the executive branch is tracking and focusing on domestic terrorism through legislation like the Domestic Terrorism Prevention Act. The federal government should collect data on domestic terrorism and provide for training for law enforcement on best practices.

Hate crimes laws can also be improved. Five states still don't even have a hate crimes law on their books. Many other states have significant gaps or weaknesses in their laws.

We also need to address our broken hate crimes reporting system because it is woeful. Hate crimes are significantly underreported to the FBI because of victims not coming forward or by law enforcement agencies failing to report hate crimes. This, too, must be addressed.

We can and must do more to counter this growing threat of extremism. We can promote anti-bias and civic education programmes. We can promote programmes within communities to counter extremist propaganda and recruiting. We can help educate the technology sector about the need to combat hate and extremism on its platforms.

We can't solve extremism. But there is so much more we should do to make sure the people who died at the hands of extremists in 2018 – and those who died before them – did not perish in vain. We can do better.

24 January 2019

Female terrorism is nothing new, but we need to understand its motives

By Yasmin Alibhai Brown

Safaa Boular, 18, was found guilty earlier this week of plotting a terrorist attack in London. Her older sister Rizlaine, 22, and 44-year-old mother, Mina, had already admitted to being part of an Isis-inspired plot to blow up landmarks across the capital.

A female terrorist cell feels both improbable and discombobulating. We are quick to assume that the guilty are puppets, their strings being pulled by some beardy puppeteer.

In this case, Safaa was, indeed, encouraged by Naweed Hussain, an Isis recruiter that she got close to online and "married" without them ever meeting. But before this, she had already been enticed by a Syrian woman to join the caliphate.

Thousands of Muslim girls and women are becoming radicalised and, in turn, radicalisers. Secret circles meet to discuss their hatred of the West. Most go no further – though their views are truly disturbing – but some then embrace violent jihadism. There is a long history of women joining guerrilla movements and terrorist campaigns, and, of course, wars.

Women can be brutal too

I went to the recording of the first of the BBC's Reith Lectures on Monday night. This year, the speaker was Margaret MacMillan, a professor of history at Oxford and an expert on international conflicts and resolutions. Someone in the audience asked if the world would be safer and more settled if women were in charge.

"No," replied the cool and rational Ms MacMillan, who went on to name famously belligerent lady leaders: India's Indira Gandhi, Israel's Golda Meir, our own Margaret Thatcher and Sri Lanka's Sirimavo Bandaranaike. Some women can be vicious, violent, cruel, subversive and destructive. Only fools and febrile man-haters believe that female humans are naturally born to be always kind and nurturing. According to Simon Webb, the author of *The Suffragette Bombers: Britain's Forgotten Terrorists*, in the years leading up to the First World War suffragette activists planted explosive devices in Westminster Abbey, St Paul's Cathedral, the Bank of England, the National Gallery, railway stations and many other locations. People got hurt. They also invented the letter bomb; designed to maim or kill those with whom they disagreed.

One of their first bomb attacks was on the home of the Chancellor of the Exchequer, David Lloyd George. The bomber was Emily Davison, who later died beneath the hooves of King George V's horse at the 1913 Epsom Derby.

The Palestinian liberationist Leila Khaled helped to hijack a plane in 1969. In 1987, Kim Hyon-hui, a North Korean zealot, placed a bomb on a South Korean airliner which killed 117 people. People thought she was too beautiful to be a terrorist. She now lives in hiding in South Korea.

There have been female terrorists or freedom fighters across Latin America, in Sri Lanka, in Kenya and, of course, South Africa during apartheid. Among today's most dangerous neo-Nazis across the West are white women of all classes.

Them and us

This is why we should not be unduly shocked by female Muslim terrorism. We should, instead, try to work out why they do what they do. Unlike, say, Khaled or Davison, they appear to have no comprehensible political aims or grievances, although clearly they feel driven to hurt and harm fellow citizens and the state.

It is telling that Safaa Boular started her journey into darkness following the Paris attacks in 2015. She wanted to find out why 'people do the things they do'. So do we.

I believe that some of this is to do with being taught from early childhood the ideas of "them" and "us", the "impure" and the "pure". Until the 1980s, western Muslims were comfortable being both. There was an internal integration of the self. But Saudi Arabian imams and books launched an assault on that dual sense of being, and women and girls were particularly targeted. A separatist mind-set and a singular religious identity became the new norm. A small minority now takes this identification to extremes.

Experts also suggest some recruits are simply breaking out of their gender roles in society in the most dramatic way. Romance, glamour and family narratives must play a part too. All of them were present in the case of Safaa Boular. What is missing is any information on the preconditions for distorted behaviours.

Was she despondent? Did she want more freedom? Did she feel misunderstood or unwanted by relatives or schoolmates? Was she an immature 17-year-old at the time, or a teenager weighed down by adult concerns? Is she evil, easily led, twisted or unintelligent?

If trained and trusted psychologists were to work patiently with such incarcerated female terrorists, we might discover why they were drawn to nihilism and brutality. Our state needs to be more emotionally literate and less gung-ho. The Home Secretary Sajid Javid, who has announced yet more anti-terrorism strategies, doesn't get that. More's the pity.

5 June 2018

What are the signs of radicalisation?

As young people go through a process of testing and developing their identity, they may be particularly vulnerable to being groomed or radicalised, either face-to-face or online.

Signs of radicalisation

Very few people that have extremist ideologies become involved in violent activity. However, it is important to consider the following points contextualised to what you know about the individual.

Do they ...

- Advocate extremist messages
- Access extremist literature and imagery
- Show an interest in and sympathy to extremist causes
- Glorify violence
- Refuse to listen to different points of view
- Feel persecuted
- Own additional mobile phones or devices
- Spend an increasing amount of time on the internet. This may be in secret or they may have more than one online identity.

Have they...

- Changed their friendship group or associate with people who hold extremist beliefs

- Lost interest in previous activities
- Changed behaviours and beliefs
- Changed their appearance
- Become increasingly argumentative and abusive to others
- Become disengaged from their studies.

How schools can help when they are concerned about radicalisation

Radicalisation is a gradual process that happens over time, making it possible to intervene and steer people away from being drawn into terrorism. If you come into regular contact with children and young people, you can help to identify patterns of behaviour that can show whether a person is engaged, is intent on causing harm or capable of committing violence.

In 2016/17, a total of 6,093 individuals were referred due to concerns that they were vulnerable to being drawn into terrorism. 1,976 of those were referred via the education sector.

1 November 2019

The martyrdom mindset: what leads people to decide to become suicide terrorists?

The first suicide bomb attack was carried out in Russia in 1881. What has since led so many people to this horrifying form of terrorism?

By Robert Verkaik

Among the multitude of videos uploaded to the internet in the early years of the war in Syria, it is hard to forget the smiling face of Abdul Waheed Majeed, pictured chatting with his friends before calmly climbing into the cab of an armour-plated lorry.

Forty minutes later, the home-made film picks up the Mad Max-style adapted vehicle trundling along the main road, heading straight for the front gates of Aleppo prison where hundreds of opponents of the Assad regime are being held.

Bullets bounce off the truck's armour as the guards suddenly realise Majeed's true intention. But their efforts are to no avail. A few seconds later a huge explosion rocks the landscape and the prison walls are breached, allowing dozens of jihadi prisoners to escape.

In Crawley, West Sussex, where Abdul Waheed Majeed, a 41-year-old father of three, had lived before leaving to join Isis, his family was inconsolable. Why did this peaceful father, son and brother leave his home in 2014 to become the first British suicide bomber in the Syrian conflict?

Perhaps only Majeed will ever be able to answer this question.

Roots beyond Islamic extremism

The appalling death toll in victims of suicide attacks across the Middle East has forged an indelible link between Islamist terrorism and weaponised self-sacrifice.

Last year there were nearly 300 suicide attacks killing almost 3,000 people and injuring 5,000 more. A total of 505 terrorists, including 84 women, participated in these car bombs, shootings and stabbings. More than half were carried out by Isis, in Syria, Iraq and Egypt.

Nine Islamist suicide bombers, eight men and one woman – all well-educated and from wealthy families – are thought to have carried out the attacks in Sri Lanka on Easter Sunday that killed at least 253 people.

The association between the suicide attack and conflicts in the Middle East seems to have been with us forever. Yet the story of the suicide bomber did not begin in the Middle East. Nor are its origins tied to the Islamic faith.

From St Petersburg to London

The world's first suicide bomber was a Russian revolutionary named Ignaty Grinevitsky. He was a member of the People's Will, a terrorist organisation which had tried and failed on many occasions to assassinate Tsar Alexander II, the leader of Imperial Russia.

On 13 March 1881, Grinevitsky and his fellow revolutionaries were determined to finish the job.

The night before the attack, Grinevitsky wrote a martyrdom letter, carefully setting out his motives for his actions. It read: 'Alexander II must die. He will die, and with him, we, his enemies, his executioners, shall die too… How many more sacrifices will our unhappy country ask of its sons before it is liberated? It is my lot to die young, I shall not see our victory, I shall not live one day, one hour in the bright season of our triumph, but I believe that with my death I shall do all that it is my duty to do, and no one in the world can demand more of me.'

The next day, as the Tsar's carriage approached a street corner near the Catherine Canal, St Petersburg, one of the three attackers threw their bombs. But the explosions failed to penetrate the carriage, leaving Alexander unharmed.

It was only when the Tsar left the safety of the carriage to check on two of his wounded Cossack guards that Grinevitsky made his move, running forwards he launched his bomb, killing Alexander outright and leaving Grinevitsky fatally wounded.

Fast forward to 7 July 2005, when four British al-Qaeda bombers attacked the London transport system killing 52 people and injuring 700 more. The group's leader, Mohammad Sidique Khan, a 30-year-old classroom assistant and father from Beeston, killed six people when he detonated his suicide bomb on a Tube train near Edgware Road.

He too left a message for posterity. In his martyrdom he called himself a "soldier" who was waging a war against the West, adding the exhortation: "Our words are dead until we give them life with our blood."

History has looked far more kindly on Grinevitsky and the Russian assassins than it has on Khan and his cell of suicide bombers. While Grinevitsky is often described as a revolutionary who gave his life for the future of the socialist state, Khan is a cold-blooded terrorist serving a warped Islamist ideology.

But if we are to be consistent, and not give political validity to those who kill for a perceived greater cause, we must be careful to denounce all suicide attacks as acts of terrorism.

Many 'causes', one belief

In Iain Overton's new book, *The Price of Paradise*, the author traces a narrative from the first Russian suicide bombers to the industrial martyrdom units of Isis. Overton explores the emergence of the suicide attacker as a weapon of war. He describes how Japanese kamikaze – "divine wind" – suicide pilots flew their Zero fighters into the hulls of Allied shipping in the Pacific.

But he also notes that human suicide bombers were active in the region well before the kamikaze units. In fact, it was the Chinese, during the Second Sino-Japanese War, 1937 to 1945, who sent soldiers with grenades packed into their metal breastplates against the better-armed Japanese armies.

Neither was the tactic confined to Japanese and Chinese combatants. 'Less well known,' says Overton, 'is the fact that some Allied troops also undertook suicide missions during the Second World War.'

Indeed, it turns out that the first suicide pilot of the Pacific campaign was not Japanese at all, but a British flier who deliberately crashed his damaged aircraft into a Japanese transport ship off the Malaya coast.

In June 1941, during the German invasion of Russia, Soviet commanders also ordered their pilots to crash their planes into those of the Luftwaffe. One of these Soviet suicide pilots was a female pilot named Yekaterina Zelenko who brought down a Messerschmitt 109 by diving her slower fighter on to it from above. On 5 May 1990, the USSR's final leader, Mikhail Gorbachev, belatedly awarded her the title of Hero of the Soviet Union.

Overton shows that even after the Second World War inferior forces called on their soldiers to make the ultimate sacrifice, whether employed in the suicide units of the Viet Cong or the killing fields of Sri Lanka. Towards the end of the 20th

Fast facts: suicide attacks

◆ Assessing the death toll of victims of suicide bombers since the days of the Tsars, author Iain Overton calculates that 250,000 people have been killed or injured – more than all the casualties in the Battle of Gettysburg, or the first day of the Somme, or the two atomic bombs dropped on Japan in 1945.

◆ The modern phenomenon of suicide bombing is considered to have begun during the Lebanese civil war. One attacker killed 307 people, including US and French military personnel, when he drove a truck into a barracks in 1983.

◆ The ringleader of the six Easter Sunday attacks in Sri Lanka, Zahran Hashim, a radical preacher who had pledged allegiance to Isis in a video, died in a blast at the Shangri-La hotel in Colombo. The Sri Lankan authorities have blamed National Thowheed Jamath, a local Islamist extremist group, for the attacks.

◆ Sri Lanka is no stranger to deadly suicide attacks. In 1996, almost 100 people were killed by an explosion at Colombo Central Bank, in an operation carried out by the separatist Tamil Tigers group.

century, terrorist groups tried to evoke the struggle of war to legitimise the actions of the suicide bombers. As we have seen, al-Qaeda and Isis brainwashed thousands of recruits, like Khan and Majeed, to sacrifice their lives in the name of their warped interpretation of the Islamic faith.

Overton has identified a common thread which he says runs through nearly all suicide bombers' justifications – 'that for others to live in this better world to come, a sacrifice is required'. And he has gone further than most to understand the motivations of the modern day suicide bomber. He even met one – or rather a bomber who had failed to blow himself up.

A sudden realisation

In 2002, Palestinian teenager Murad Tawalbeh decided to carry out a suicide bomb attack after his friend was killed by an Israeli military sniper. He had been protesting with the teenager at an Israeli checkpoint on the West Bank when his friend was fatally shot in the chest. According to Overton, Tawalbeh's decision was a culmination of a long road of frustration in which he had been worn down by the oppression of the Israeli state.

Most of all, he told Overton, he was deeply affected by a picture of a dead baby Palestinian girl who had been killed during an Israeli attack.

One day in 2002, Tawalbeh, 19 at the time, put on his best T-shirt, kissed his family goodbye as they slept, and slipped out into the pre-dawn to meet his brother, a well-known Palestinian fighter. His brother helped him put on the suicide vest – a bulky brown contraption with a tube made of iron – crying and kissing him as he did so, says Overton.

He then took a taxi to Haifa and walked into the town's marketplace where he intended to detonate his bomb. But among the early morning commuters and shoppers, his attention was drawn to a mother and her child, a baby similar to one in the picture he carried with him.

'I started thinking,' he told Overton. 'I am here to stop the killing of babies, so I couldn't imagine myself killing another baby.' He immediately left the market and discarded his suicide vest in wasteland, but was soon picked up by Israeli security forces who found him around the town without a permit. They linked him to the bomb and he was sentenced to seven years' imprisonment. He was released in 2008.

Overton has also spent time with some of the survivors of the recent carnage. Their stories are moving and direct testimony of the pointless damage done to innocent lives.

'They share their stories in different ways,' he says. 'Some feel guilty, knowing that they survive while others fell. Some rock nervously in the telling; others talk with calm, steady voices as if they weren't even there. They speak of their children waiting for them at home; of parents nervously texting to ask where they are; of the noise of the ringing mobile phones of the dead never to be answered.'

1 May 2019

Use of the word 'radicalisation' is ballooning – and it's hiding the real causes of violence

An article from The Conversation.

THE CONVERSATION

By Rob Faure Walker PhD Candidate and Tutor in MA Education, UCL

The term "radicalisation" recently started appearing as an explanation for US high school shootings in my newsfeeds. In an article titled "Call the Florida shooting what it is: terrorism", *Teen Vogue* explores the murderer's connections to white supremacy and claims that "the source of their radicalisation" is the "main question currently plaguing our society".

This was the first time that I had noticed that the US media were using "radicalisation" as an explanation for this horrendous phenomenon. Researching the emergence of a violent discourse of radicalisation and extremism for my PhD and compiling the Prevent digest – a monthly summary of news on the UK government's counter-terrorism Prevent strategy – tends to keep me abreast of new uses of the word. It also leaves me concerned when I see them. Here's why.

Today, "radicalisation" may appear to be a common-sense explanation for acts of political violence, but this has not always been the case. You'll struggle to find the word in contemporary explanations for 9/11. One notable example of this is in the philosopher Giovanna Borradori's book of dialogues with Jurgen Habermas and Jacques Derrida in the weeks following the attacks on the Twin Towers. In their extensive discussion of the causes of this tragedy and of terrorism more generally, they fail to mention "radicalisation" at all. On reflection, this isn't so surprising. This iconic event was after all Ground Zero for the War on Terror, the first war to focus on "radicalisation".

The cognitive linguist and philosopher George Lakoff has written extensively on why the language we use to frame political debates matters. He explains why at the opening of his book, *Don't Think of an Elephant!:*

> *'Frames are mental structures that shape the way we see the world. As a result, they shape the goals we seek, the plans we make, the way we act, and what counts as a good or bad outcome of our actions. In politics our frames shape our social policies and the institutions we form to carry out policies. To change our frames is to change all of this. Reframing is social change.'*

"Radicalisation" is such a common word now that it may appear as if we have always used it. But this has not always been the case – and our use of it is reframing how we see many issues. It used to be so rare in political explanations that it only appears 14 times in the UK's parliamentary record between 1803 and 2005. In the following decade it appeared 1,355 times.

The UK parliament now holds debates on the subjects of "radicalisation" and "anti-radicalisation programmes".

The emergence and proliferation of "radicalisation" is explained by Peter Neumann, Director of the International Centre for the Study of Radicalisation. Neumann has argued that after 9/11 "it suddenly became very difficult to talk about the 'roots of terrorism', which some commentators claimed was an effort to excuse and justify the killing of innocent civilians".

In response, Neumann tells us that 'experts and officials started referring to the idea of "radicalisation" whenever they wanted to talk about "what goes on before the bomb goes off".' Neumann shows us that the word "radicalisation" emerged as an attempt to reframe the causes of terrorism.

Since then, "radicalisation" has been used to justify the incursion of the security services into schools and hospitals by highly controversial strategies. Strategies such as Prevent, which target so-called "radicalisation", have faced much opposition for their apparent racial bias. I have written about the possibility that they might actually promote rather than prevent violence. It has also been well documented that there is little or no evidence base for these strategies.

So what happens when we frame the many possible causes of violence as "radicalisation"? The linguist Norman Fairclough refers to describing disparate processes as a single entity as "nominalization" in his book on analysing discourse. He warns that this tendency risks mystifying the causes of and denying human agency to the phenomenon described. If we take heed of Fairclough's warning, could this nominalisation of "radicalisation" be hiding the causes of violence?

When the word "radicalisation" gets co-opted to describe a teenager who had access to an assault rifle and who was driven to mass murder by many known and unknown factors, the issue is reframed. The resulting debate enables right-wing media outlets to focus on the regulation of social media rather than controlling children's access to assault rifles. A very real cause of the death of children, as described by their classmates , is hidden by a more abstract process.

As a fresh example of reframing, it is not hard to see how "radicalisation" might skew the gun control debate. Perhaps it should give us pause to question the extent to which "radicalisation" has led the UK government to focus on young children as terrorist threats and to also call for the regulation of social media.

8 March 2018

More than 150 children subject of court proceedings amid fears they are being radicalised by extremists

By Ellie Cullen PA & Kirsty Bosley

More than 150 children have been have involved in care proceedings in the UK since 2013 over concerns they were in danger of being radicalised, a report has said.

The study, by think tank the Henry Jackson Society, found the family courts were often powerless to take steps to protect the welfare of the youngsters, even when they were aware that the parents involved had extremist mindsets.

Urgent reform is needed in the face of a potential "wave" of women who joined Islamic State returning to the UK with their children, the report's author warned.

It comes as the debate rages on over what should happen to Shamima Begum, the 19-year-old who fled east London in 2015 to join IS and now wants to return to Britain with her baby son.

Nikita Malik, director of the Centre on Radicalisation and Terrorism and the report's author, said: "The UK faces a real and imminent prospect of a wave of women from Islamic State returning to the UK with babies and children in tow. They return to a family courts system that is not currently up to the task of handling the serious challenges of extremism.

"The Family Courts requires urgent reform to ensure that they are procedurally fit for this emergent risk.

"Failure to see such reform could mean the children of extremists remain in the hands of their potentially dangerous parents."

The study found a number of inconsistencies in the way children at risk of radicalisation were dealt with, as some were put under travel restrictions, some were made wards of court or put in the care of other family members, and in other cases charges against the family were dropped.

There was also "uncertainty" over the concepts of radicalisation and extremism themselves, it warned.

Twenty of the 156 cases before the courts between 2013 and 2018 were analysed in more detail, with 55% of cases having links to Al-Muhajiroun, the banned group founded by Anjem Choudary.

Three main causes were identified for pushing youngsters towards radicalisation, including being taken out of school, having a family with a history of extremist activity or coming from a broken home.

A total of 67% of families involved in the cases had a history of domestic abuse or a history of wider criminal conduct, almost 20% of the children involved were homeschooled, while 38% of families contained children absent from school.

The report also concluded that girls who travel to the so-called caliphate make their own decisions, more so than boys.

The boys tended to join Islamic State under the influence of their families, whereas girls were more active and independent in seeking out extremist material, it said.

"The cases in the report are unique, in that the threat to children is ideological as well as physical," said Ms Malik.

"When courts act in these cases, they must settle upon a course of action which not only protects the child from harm, but protects them from becoming a person who does harm to themselves or others in the future."

Lord Carlile, former independent reviewer of terrorism legislation, said it was apparent that the family court was not always able to "take the appropriate steps to protect" children in such cases.

"The report stimulates a necessary and open discussion about how we tackle this, including what additional powers are needed to safeguard children whose lives may be ruined by the extremist ideas and intentions of parents and others close to the family," he said.

21 February 2019

The radicalisation of Shamima Begum is a problem made in Britain

By Sunder Katwala, Director of British Future

Shamima Begum made a terrible decision when she chose to go to Syria to join Islamic State, where she married a fighter. Because she was only a 15-year-old girl when she was radicalised by a murderous death cult, many people are torn by competing intuitions when considering the case. Begum has seen terrible things that most of us will never experience – yet she went to champion and support those carrying them out. She has seen two of her children die by the age of 19, and her newborn baby is an innocent born into the least auspicious of circumstances.

Yet when Begum declares herself unfazed by the brutality of ISIS putting heads on spikes in Syria, and justifies the murder of children who went to a pop concert in Manchester with their families, it is no surprise that most people feel Britain would be better off if she was never to return.

Home Secretary Sajid Javid's decision to try to strip Begum of her citizenship will prove broadly popular with the public, though it appears much less likely to be judged lawful if and when that question is tested in court.

The Home Office believes the decision can be made on the basis that she may hold, or be eligible for, Bangladeshi citizenship. Yet Bangladesh is clear that she is not a citizen – and unsurprisingly regards the radicalisation of Shamima Begum as a British problem, not one to be dumped on Bangladesh. This country would hardly take in somebody with extreme and radicalised views, who had never been here, having grown up in America, Bangladesh or Canada with a parental link to this country.

Even if his move appears likely to be blocked, Javid may still feel that it would have been right to send a message about British citizenship being incompatible with joining an extreme terrorist group.

Most people do understand that citizenship is about responsibilities as well as rights – because the rights we enjoy depend on a respect for the rights of others. The sense of a social contract with our fellow citizens is betrayed by Begum's support of Daesh – as it was broken by those who spied on their country for the Soviet Union, or mounted and supported campaigns of terror and violence, whether from the IRA or Daesh.

Yet the decision also risks badly damaging one of the core principles of citizenship. Strong citizenship societies believe in equal citizenship and so strive to come ever closer to upholding the ideal that those who choose to become Canadian or American or British have a similar status to everyone else in the club that they join. Yet Sajid Javid's decision indicates an increasingly expansive approach to entrenching a two-tier approach to British citizenship.

Here it is not only dual nationals who can lose their citizenship, or those who become naturalised. Javid's decision appears to propose a new principle – that those who are eligible for another citizenship could see their British citizenship revoked.

Who is and is not affected would depend on the lottery of national citizenship rules, but that impact would not be felt equally across society. I was surprised to discover that the Irish government considers me automatically Irish – because my Irish mother was born in Cork – whether I apply for a passport or not, whereas those like my children, who qualify by descent via a grandparent, need to register to be eligible. If eligibility were the only criterion, this would be likely to affect the majority of British citizens from ethnic and faith minorities – and a much smaller group of white British peers. It will affect many more Britons with parentage and family ties to Commonwealth countries, along with Poland, Ireland or Israel.

That implication of the Home Secretary's effort has drawn criticism from an unusually broad spectrum of views. Maajid Nawaz of the Quilliam Foundation suggests that the move is 'worse than anything Donald Trump has done', because it makes second-class citizens of those whose parents have another heritage. 'If citizenship is revocable for people like me, it was never citizenship to begin with', but more like a mere visa, he wrote in a social media post.

Telling IRA terrorists that the British state would revoke their rights to be British would have been an own goal, given that their central claim was the illegitimacy of Britain's presence in Northern Ireland. (I doubt anybody thought of telling the Ulster Volunteer Force that Britain intended to render them Irish, which might have been a stronger deterrent, though there would have been no reason for Dublin to play along.) Islamist extremism remains a toxic threat, both in the direct danger it poses to the safety of us all, and in its efforts to form a symbiotic relationship with supposedly opposing extremists on the far right to spread a shared message that Muslims can never be fully part of British society.

If the radicalisation of Shamima Begum was a problem made in Britain, so the question we need to be asking is how we redouble our efforts to protect young people from the lure of this theocratic fascism. Hers is far from the only case. Indeed, it is the retreat of IS and the failure of the fantasies of its Caliphate which sees an increasing number of states now grappling with the difficult issues of what to do with combatants, or their families, who seek to return. Few have rejected the values that we want to share in Britain – but our response should demonstrate our confidence in the values and capacity of British justice to deal with problems which are our responsibility.

21 February 2019

Britain could deradicalise Shamima Begum – with compassion

By Dawn Foster

The CCTV images of the three teenage girls Shamima Begum, Kadiza Sultana and Amira Abase passing through Gatwick airport four years ago en route to join the Islamic State "caliphate" were shocking for much of the British public. That Isis was radicalising people online was no surprise, but the fact these three girls were as young as 15 and from the same academy school in Bethnal Green, east London, cast the risks of radicalisation closer to home.

The discredited counter-radicalisation strategy, Prevent, was meant to stem the recruitment of "homegrown" terrorists, including those recruited into the far right, but has disproportionately focused on Islamist extremism without yielding any significant concrete results. Last year, for example, an essay by the late Marxist political theorist Norman Geras on the political uses of violence was deemed so dangerous under the Prevent programme that Reading University students were warned not to leave it lying around where it could be seen "by those who are not prepared to view it". The university flagged the text as an extremist piece of work that should only be read in a secure setting. Yet while curtailing academic freedom, the scheme, launched by Labour in 2003 but expanded by the coalition in 2011, appears to have successfully identified or stopped very few individuals who would otherwise have left the country to join Isis. It emerged on Monday that another Bethnal Green teenager trying to get to Syria was hauled off a flight to Turkey in December 2014 but never prosecuted – a slip that may have made it easier for the other three to make their journey the following year. It is difficult to argue that we have achieved the right balance when heavy-handed surveillance has been ushered into classrooms, yet we failed to notice 15-year-old girls flying to Turkey unaccompanied.

Four years on, Sultana has reportedly died in an airstrike, Abase's whereabouts are unknown and Begum, who last week turned up in a Syrian refugee camp, was separated from her jihadi husband and has now given birth to a third child. She is expressing a wish to return home, and her lawyer states that she is psychologically damaged as a result of four years with the terrorist group – though she expresses no regret for joining.

Her family have offered to raise the child, away from the ideology that has characterised her four years abroad. Her case has prompted fierce debate, with the home secretary, Sajid Javid, saying he will 'not hesitate to prevent' the return of British citizens who joined Isis in Iraq and Syria. Among the general public too there has been a chorus of calls for the lack of mercy shown to Isis victims to be extended to Begum and her newborn son. On one BBC radio show, the presenter expressed alarm at the bloodthirsty fate so many callers wished on the teenager and her baby.

One suggested she be left to 'rot in a cage'; none were able to explain how the cruelty that they held in contempt when enacted by Isis would be justified if carried out by British forces.

The compassionate course to take would be to let Begum return home, and accept that an eye for an eye turns the whole world blind and that the public can still be protected if she is dealt with in the UK. Begum herself has said she is happy to face prison, and while she does not yet express any open regret for her actions, she appears aware that she must face consequences. 'I actually do support some British values and I am willing to go back to the UK and settle back again and rehabilitate,' she told the BBC on Monday. Rendering Begum stateless would simply allow her recruiters to cast the British state in disparaging terms. She admits she was used as an Isis poster girl, so preventing her – and especially her baby – from returning would be a propaganda boon for Isis when its powers are otherwise waning.

Even if you do not accept human empathy as a base level for the state's response you must appreciate the need to begin the process of "deradicalisation". I believe any attempt at helping Begum has to meet her part-way: she has expressed a wish to come home and face the consequences, and this will involve some commitment on her part. But we must also acknowledge the failures of an anti-radicalisation strategy that has left many young Muslims feeling victimised, isolated and perhaps even more vulnerable to online groomers.

The current system isn't working. Treating at-risk young people as individual cases and doing so with compassion – starting with Begum – has to offer a better way forward.

18 February 2019

RADICALISING OUR CHILDREN: An analysis of family court cases of British children at risk of radicalisation, 2013–2018

A summary.

By Nikita Malik

> ● **Over 156 children involved in family court cases in which extremism was cited**
>
> ● **48% of families in extremism proceedings had one member join IS**

A t least 156 children have been involved in family court cases in which concerns over extremism or radicalisation have been cited, according to a new study released by the Henry Jackson Society. Of the cases examined, the think tank found that 48% of families had one family member or more who joined IS. Nikita Malik, Director of the Centre on Radicalisation and Terrorism and the report's author, today warns that the UK's courts are not currently up to the task of handling a wave of women who joined the 'caliphate' returning with their children.

The report concludes that the family court is frequently powerless to take steps to protect the welfare of children, even when the counter-terrorism division is aware that parents involved are often terrorists with extremist mindsets. The former Independent Reviewer of Terrorism Legislation, Lord Carlile, welcomed the report, and stated it is 'apparent that the family court is not always able to take the appropriate steps to protect' the children of extremists. Meanwhile, Tim Loughton MP, the former Children's Minister, stressed that the Family Courts require 'better protocols, guidance and support' to deal with this 'increasingly urgent part of their role'.

Contrary to claims the girls of Islamic State were vulnerable brides, the report finds that, far more so than boys, girls who travel to the 'caliphate' made their own decisions. The author concludes that boys tended to join Islamic State under the influence of their families, whereas girls were more active and independent in seeking out extremist material – often online. All of the girls in cases analysed by the study who had self-radicalised were motivated in part by the possibility of marriage to a person of their choice.

The study, which qualitatively analyses the 20 cases with the most comprehensive court records over recent years, also found that:

◆ 55% of cases had links to Al-Muhajiroun, the banned group founded by Anjem Choudary.

◆ 67% of families had a history of domestic abuse or a history of wider criminal conduct.

◆ Almost 20% of the children involved were home-schooled; while, 38% families contained children absent from school.

◆ In cases where gender was known, 64% of children involved in court actions were boys.

The report calls for a bespoke set of powers for judges to use in cases of extremism involving children. Citing the high burden of proof required for the more traditional option of care orders, the report argues that the powers imbued with wardship have proved more suitable in many cases, to meet the growing and pertinent challenge of countering radicalisation.

> *'The UK faces a real and imminent prospect of a wave of women from Islamic State returning to the UK with babies and children in tow. They return to a family courts system that is not currently up to the task of handling the serious challenges of extremism.*
>
> *The Family Courts require urgent reform to ensure that they are procedurally fit for this emergent risk. Failure to see such reform could mean the children of extremists remain in the hands of their potentially dangerous parents.*
>
> *The cases in the report are unique, in that the threat to children is ideological as well as physical. When courts act in these cases, they must settle upon a course of action which not only protects the child from harm, but protects them from becoming a person who does harm to themselves or others in the future.'*

– **Nikita Malik,** Director of the Centre on Radicalisation and Terrorism at the Henry Jacskon Society

20 February 2019

Radicalised children pose security 'risk' in Germany: report

Exposure of minors to radical Islam is 'alarming', German authorities warn.

By Maxime Schlee

German authorities have warned that several hundred children are at risk of Islamic radicalisation and pose a 'not negligible' risk to security.

Children and adolescents growing up in families that follow radical Islamist teachings are "raised with an extremist worldview that legitimizes violence toward others and belittles those who do not belong to their group," according to an analysis by Germany's Federal Office for the Protection of the Constitution.

Children in this group show signs of "faster, earlier and more likely radicalization," according to the report, a copy of which was seen by newspapers belonging to the Funke media group.

The exposure of minors to radical Islam is "alarming" and poses a "challenge" for the years ahead, Hans-Georg Maaßen, the president of the Office for the Protection of the Constitution, told the media group.

Maaßen warned in December last year that children and women returning to Germany from territories held by the terror group Islamic State posed a threat to German security. The body's latest report specifies that the threat also exists within an estimated 'low three-figure number' of families living in Germany who have not travelled to Syria or Iraq.

The report has prompted members of Chancellor Angela Merkel's ruling Christian Democrats to call for loosening regulations that prevent the body from surveilling children under the age of 14.

"This is not about criminalising young people under 14 but defending against considerable risks in our country, for example through Islamist terrorism, which is also using children," CDU security expert Patrick Sensburg said.

6 August 2018

French counter-terrorism targets climate activists

By Natalie Sauer

When Marion Esnault and comrades began removing portraits of president Emmanuel Macron from the walls of town halls across France they expected to get into trouble.

But it has now emerged that their protest – involving up to 27 portraits so far – against what they say is Macron's failure of climate leadership, has become the target of an investigation involving France's Bureau de la Lutte Anti-terroriste (Blat), the office of counter-terrorism operations.

In correspondence leaked online, and reported by environmental publication *Reporterre*, Marc de Tarlé, deputy director of the judicial police, urged police forces to 'counter this phenomenon' by contacting the Bureau de la Lutte Anti-terroriste (Blat), France's office of counter-terrorism operations, and asking for help to investigate the group, known as ANV-COP21 (Non-Violent Action COP21).

Offences

It was unclear what assistance the Blat are expected to give police. But Marion Esnault, an activist who has taken down three portraits of Macron in Paris, told Climate Home News that the involvement of an agency self-described as 'specifically concerned with the prevention and repression of terrorism acts', was disturbing.

According to ANV-COP21, 276 activists have taken part in actions since they began in February. In response, police

have prosecuted 20 people, detained 22 people and carried out 16 police searches.

'We had thought that the repression we'd faced until now – all of the police custodies, the police searches, and the four trials with many incriminated activists – was out of proportion for a symbolic action,' said Esnault. 'But for them now to call on the Blat, it's beyond disproportion. There are no words. We are considered terrorists when we're citizens aware of the climate crisis and the current ecological catastrophe.'

Esnault said she understood certain actions risked prosecution, such as when Greenpeace activists entered nuclear power stations. 'It's more surprising to see activists who enter townhalls to take down portraits of Macron, demanding that he lead more ambitious climate policy, end up with trials and police custodies,' she said.

'It isn't normal to resort to anti-terrorist units in order to pursue activists whose acts threaten neither the security nor the integrity of the state,' Alexandre Faro, a lawyer representing members of ANV-COP21, told *Reporterre*. 'These are theft charges, thus common-law offences: what is the point of resorting to the office of anti-terrorist operations?'

Green scare

The gendarmerie brushed off the correspondence, telling Reporterre that 'just because the BLAT is involved doesn't mean that it'll take on exceptional proportions'. The letter

wasn't classified, they said, pointing out the 'routine' tag pinned to the top of the message. The police force did not respond to questions from CHN.

Tarlé also instructed police forces to encourage mayors or state prefects to press charges against activists and 'ensure that a judicial investigation be systematically carried out for aggravated robbery'.

The incident comes amid a hardening of responses from governments across Western Europe to protest groups calling for a faster response to climate change.

Heather Albarrro, an associate lecturer in political ecology at Nottingham Trent University, said there were signs of a resurgence of "green scare" – a phenomenon in the mid-2000s during which the US government persecuted environmental activists. At its height, the FBI labelled the Earth Liberation Front as the nation's lead domestic terrorist threat.

'The question of the green scare resurgence – maybe it's not in full force as it was in previous decades,' Albarro told Climate Home News. 'But then again, with the increasing severity of things like climate change and increasing desperation of some of these more radical strands, you might see more clamping down.'

Extremism

Albarro said the key message of the green scare was that authorities 'weren't clamping down on these activists

because they were a threat to life per se. What they are is a threat to the status quo in the sense of growth-oriented capitalism'.

In February, high commissioner of human rights Michelle Bachelet recommended the UN investigate France for excessive use of force by police forces against the gilets jaunes.

Outside France, the German government deployed one of the largest police forces since WWII to arrest activists occupying Hambach forest in an effort to keep coal giant RWE at bay. One person died in an accident, according to climate campaign group 350.org.

Meanwhile, the British government's extremism analysis unit has produced a report called *Leftwing Activism and Extremism in the UK*, according a February investigation by *The Guardian*.

Part of 21 reports designed to inform on extremism, including Islamist and far-right wing extremism, the document comes four years after it was revealed that an extremist database included politicians and activists. The political activities of Jenny Jones, a London assembly member, and Green Party councillor Ian Driver were recorded.

4 April 2019

Prevent: UK's Counter Terrorism Strategy

Like CONTEST as a whole, Prevent now addresses radicalisation to all forms of terrorism. At the same time integration projects are no longer being securitised, as they were before.

Success in Prevent in CONTEST will mean that:

◆ There is a reduction in support for terrorism of all kinds and in states overseas whose security most impacts the UK

◆ There is more effective challenge to those extremists whose views are shared by terrorist organisations and used by terrorists to legitimise violence, and

◆ There is more challenge to and isolation of extremists and terrorists operating on the internet.

What is Prevent?

Prevent is one part of the UK's CONTEST Counter Terrorism Strategy. It includes four sections:

◆ Pursue: to stop terrorist attacks

◆ Prevent: to stop people becoming terrorists or supporting terrorism

◆ Protect: to strengthen protection against a terrorist attack, and

◆ Prepare: to mitigate the impact of a terrorist attack.

Prevent is unique in that it involves all parts of Government such as the Home Office, the Cabinet Office, the Foreign and Commonwealth Office and the Department for International Development.

When was Prevent released?

The revised Prevent Strategy was released in June 2011 with the full CONTEST Strategy being released in July 2011. These are the third versions of both strategies.

Why now?

The need for an up-to-date strategy is reflected in both the British threat level, where there is continuing risk of a terrorist attack (for example: Substantial for England but Severe for Northern Ireland) and the change in government.

The new Prevent Strategy was released by the Coalition Government. It is a full reworking of the old strategy and has been brought up-to-date to reflect changed circumstances, such as value for money (VfM) and the localism agenda.

UK's CONTEST Counter Terrorism Strategy

Prevent is a key part of the Contest Counter Terrorism Strategy. The Government has now changed both its scope and its focus in this area.

What are the key elements of the Strategy?

Prevent addresses three distinct themes. These are:

1) Challenging the ideology that supports terrorism and those who promote it

All terrorist groups have an ideology. Promoting that ideology, frequently on the internet, facilitates radicalisation and recruitment. A fundamental part of Prevent lies in challenging their ideology and disrupting the ability of terrorists to promote it.

2) Protecting vulnerable people

Radicalisation is usually a process not an event. During that process it is possible to intervene to prevent vulnerable people being drawn into terrorist-related activity. There are some analogies between this work and other forms of crime prevention.

3) Supporting sectors and institutions where there are risks of radicalisation

A wide range of sectors are helping to prevent people becoming terrorists or supporting terrorism. The way Government works with particular sectors will vary. Priority areas include education, faith, health, criminal justice and charities. The internet is also included as a theme running through the Strategy.

The main focus is on Al-Qaida-inspired terrorism, though other types are covered.

www.esrc.ukri.org

Security and terrorism in numbers

An extract from STATE OF HATE 2019 report.

The Prevent strategy forms part of the Government's wider counter-terrorism strategy, known as CONTEST. According to the Government, Prevent aims to safeguard people from becoming terrorists or supporting terrorism.

If a member of the public, or someone working with the public has a concern about a person they know who may be radicalised, they can raise these concerns with their local authority safeguarding team or the police for an assessment.

The Channel programme in England and Wales is a voluntary initiative that provides a multi-agency approach to support people vulnerable to being drawn into terrorism.

Prevent has faced fierce criticism since its inception, particularly from the Muslim community, and last month the Government announced an independent review.

PREVENT AND CHANNEL

In 2017/18, a total of **7,318** individuals were subject to a referral due to concerns that they were vulnerable to being drawn into terrorism.
Of these:

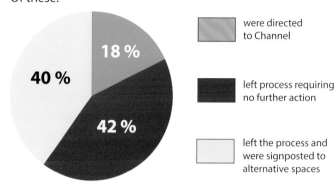

- were directed to Channel — 18 %
- left process requiring no further action — 42 %
- left the process and were signposted to alternative spaces — 40 %

AGE
PREVENT REFERRALS

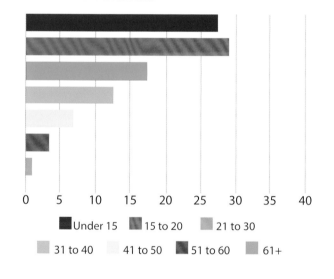

Legend:
- Under 15
- 15 to 20
- 21 to 30
- 31 to 40
- 41 to 50
- 51 to 60
- 61+

1,314 people who were directed to Channel. Of these:

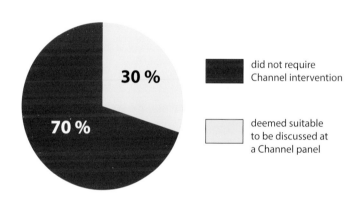

- did not require Channel intervention — 70 %
- deemed suitable to be discussed at a Channel panel — 30 %

TYPE OF CONCERN

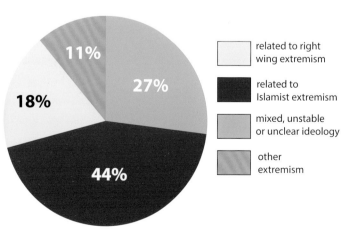

- related to right wing extremism — 18%
- related to Islamist extremism — 44%
- mixed, unstable or unclear ideology — 27%
- other extremism — 11%

394 individuals received Channel support following a Channel panel.
Of these:

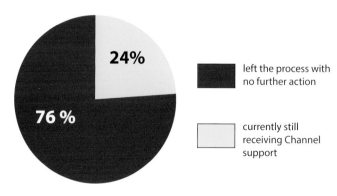

- left the process with no further action — 76 %
- currently still receiving Channel support — 24%

There were 317 arrests for terrorism-related activity in the year ending 30 September 2018, a decrease of 31% compared with the 462 arrests in the previous year, according to Home Office statistics.

The fall was largely due to the exceptionally high numbers of people arrested after the terrorist attacks in London and Manchester in 2017.

Of the 317 arrests for terrorism-related activity:

◆ 113 (36%) resulted in a charge, of which 85 were terrorism-related

◆ 165 (52%) people arrested were released without charge

◆ 17 (5%) persons were released on bail pending further investigation

◆ 20 (6%) faced alternative action

◆ two cases were pending at the time of data provision

Of the 85 persons charged with a terrorism-related offence, 37 had been prosecuted, all of whom had been convicted. A total of 47 people were awaiting prosecution and one was not proceeded against.

At the end of September 2018, there were 224 persons in custody in Great Britain for terrorism-related offences, an increase of 5% on the previous year. The vast majority (186 – 83%) had been convicted, with the remaining 38 (17%) on remand awaiting trial.

However, the convictions have not been without controversy. In December, 15 people were convicted under terrorist legislation after blocking the takeoff of an immigration removal charter flight at Stansted airport. They and their supporters have claimed that this is an appalling abuse of

OF THE 224 PRISONERS IN CUSTODY

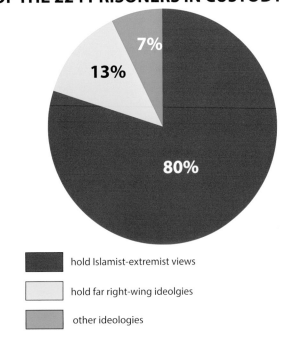

7%

13%

80%

■ hold Islamist-extremist views

□ hold far right-wing ideolgies

■ other ideologies

the system and an 'unprecedented crackdown on the right to protest'.

The Guardian has estimated that 40% of those convicted of terror-related offences between 2007 and 2016 would have been eligible for release by the end of 2018.

17 February 2019

www.hopenothate.org.uk

Prevent: anti-terror strategy condemned as "toxic brand"

Former senior police officer says Muslims see UK's counter-terror programme as form of spying

A former senior Muslim police officer has described the government's Prevent strategy, intended to stop people becoming terrorists, as a "toxic brand".

Dal Babu, who retired as a chief superintendent with the Metropolitan Police two years ago, said many Muslims did not trust the programme and saw it as a form of spying.

Police counter-terrorism units are mainly white, with a lack of knowledge about issues of race and Islam, he said.

One senior officer did not know the difference between Sunni and Shia Muslims – a lack of knowledge 'amplified considerably' with more junior officers, he added.

Babu suggested authorities were caught unaware in cases such as the three London schoolgirls who travelled to Syria to join Islamic State (IS).

'Sadly, Prevent has become a toxic brand and most Muslims are suspicious of what Prevent is doing,' he told the BBC.

'This is unfortunate but a reality and the government needs to develop a strategy to safeguard vulnerable children who are being groomed by IS.'

In light of the militant group's "endless stream" of propaganda and 3,000-plus recruits from Europe, BBC security correspondent Frank Gardner questioned on Friday whether the strategy is failing.

The scheme, which has an annual budget of £40m, was described as "counterproductive" by Aminul Hoque, a lecturer and author on British Islamic identity at the University of London.

'If the idea was to understand the roots of extremism, the roots of radicalisation, by putting a magnifying glass across the Muslim communities of Great Britain, what has happened is that has widened the schism between the "Muslim" us and the British "other",' he said.

The Home Office says 75,000 pieces of 'unlawful terrorist material' have been removed from the internet since 2011, while 200,000 leaflets and posters warning people not to travel to Syria have been distributed with the help of mosques and faith groups. It added that 130,000 people had been trained to help identify and prevent extremism.

March 2015

Four ways social media platforms could stop the spread of hateful content in aftermath of terror attacks

THE CONVERSATION

An article from The Conversation.

By Bertie Vidgen PhD Candidate, Alan Turing Institute, University of Oxford

The deadly attack on two mosques in Christchurch, New Zealand, in which 50 people were killed and many others critically injured, was streamed live on Facebook by the man accused of carrying it out. It was then quickly shared across social media platforms.

Versions of the livestream attack video stayed online for a worrying amount of time. A report by *The Guardian* found that one video stayed on Facebook for six hours and another on YouTube for three. For many, the quick and seemingly unstoppable spread of this video typifies everything that is wrong with social media: toxic, hate-filled content which goes viral and is seen by millions.

But we should avoid scapegoating the big platforms. All of them (Twitter, Facebook, YouTube, Google, Snapchat) are signed up to the European Commission's #NoPlace4Hate programme. They are committed to removing illegal hateful content within 24 hours, a time period which is likely to come down to just one hour.

Aside from anything else, they are aware of the reputational risks of being associated with terrorism and other harmful content (such as pornography, suicide, paedophilia) and are increasingly devoting considerable resources to removing it. Within 24 hours of the Christchurch attack, Facebook had banned 1.5 million versions of the attack video – of which 1.2 million it stopped from being uploaded at all.

Monitoring hateful content is always difficult and even the most advanced systems accidentally miss some. But during terrorist attacks the big platforms face particularly

significant challenges As research has shown, terrorist attacks precipitate huge spikes in online hate, overrunning platforms' reporting systems. Lots of the people who upload and share this content also know how to deceive the platforms and get round their existing checks.

So what can platforms do to take down extremist and hateful content immediately after terrorist attacks? I propose four special measures which are needed to specifically target the short-term influx of hate.

1. Adjust the sensitivity of the hate detection tools

All tools for hate detection have a margin of error. The designers have to decide how many false negatives and false positives they are happy with. False negatives are bits of content which are allowed online even though they are hateful and false positives are bits of content which are blocked even though they are non-hateful. There is always a trade off between the two when implementing any hate detection system.

The only way to truly ensure that no hateful content goes online is to ban all content from being uploaded – but this would be a mistake. Far better to adjust the sensitivity of the algorithms so that people are allowed to share content but platforms catch a lot more of the hateful stuff.

2. Enable easier takedowns

Hateful content which does get onto the big platforms, such as Twitter and Facebook, can be flagged by users. It is then sent for manual review by a content moderator, who checks it using predefined guidelines. Content moderation is a fundamentally difficult business, and the platforms aim to minimise inaccurate reviews. Often this is by using the "stick": according to some investigative journalists, moderators working on behalf of Facebook risk losing their jobs unless they maintain high moderation accuracy scores.

During attacks, platforms could introduce special procedures so that staff can quickly work through content without fear of low performance evaluation. They could also introduce temporary quarantines so that content is flagged for immediate removal but then re-examined at a later date.

3. Limit the ability of users to share

Sharing is a fundamental part of social media, and platforms actively encourage sharing both on their sites (which is crucial to their business models) and between them, as it means that none of them miss out when anything goes viral. But easy sharing also brings with it risks: research shows that extreme and hateful content is imported from niche far-right sites and dumped into the mainstream where it can quickly spread to large audiences. And during attacks it means that anything which gets past one platform's hate detection software can be quickly shared across all of the platforms.

Platforms should limit the number of times that content can be shared within their site and potentially ban shares between sites. This tactic has already been adopted by WhatsApp, which now limits the number of times content can be shared to just five.

4. Create shared databases of content

All of the big platforms have very similar guidelines on what constitutes "hate" and will be trying to take down largely the same content following attacks. Creating a shared database of hateful content would ensure that content removed from one site is automatically banned from another. This would not only avoid needless duplication but enable the platforms to quickly devote resources to the really challenging content that is hard to detect.

Removing hateful content should be seen as an industry-wide effort and not a problem each platform faces individually. Shared databases like this do also exist in a limited way but efforts need to be hugely stepped up and their scope broadened.

In the long term, platforms need to keep investing in content moderation and developing advanced systems which integrate human checks with machine learning. But there is also a pressing need for special measures to handle the short-term influx of hate following terrorist attacks.

18 March 2019

Charged for three clicks of a mouse: online crime and the new counter-terrorism bill

The Government is proposing a new counter-terrorism bill. But can it really strike a balance between liberty and security?

By Hoda Hashem

The UK has a long history of controversial counter-terrorism measures. The most recent is the proposed Counter-Terrorism and Border Security Bill 2018. Home Secretary Sajid Javid recently denied that the new laws could undermine essential rights and freedoms. Instead, he argued that the bill would strike a balance between liberty and national security.

However, some of the proposed laws could threaten this balance and potentially breach human rights if they pass unchanged.

Arrested for surfing the web?

Under section 58 of the Terrorism Act 2000, it's unlawful to possess material likely to assist a terrorist, including internet downloads. Academics and journalists conducting terrorism-related research can avoid a conviction by proving that they had a 'reasonable excuse' for accessing the material.

However, the government wants to extend this law to cover situations where someone has repeatedly viewed such material – without the need to demonstrate criminal intent.

During a presentation to the Joint Committee on Human Rights, the advocacy group Liberty recently argued that it's important not to criminalise innocent curiosity. To do so could undermine freedom of expression (Article 10 in the Human Rights Convention) which includes the right to both 'receive and impart information'.

The government's response to this argument is the 'three clicks' approach. This means they will not charge people who have only viewed potentially criminal content once or twice.

Does the 'three clicks' approach make sense?

So why can someone be innocently curious once, or even twice, but not a third time? This was a question posed by Max Hill QC, the Independent Reviewer of Terrorism Legislation. During parliamentary discussions of the bill, Sajid Javid appeared to accept the critique's validity. 'I am not pretending there is something magical about the number three,' he conceded.

The Home Secretary stated that the police and Crown Prosecution Service would be given discretion over who to

prosecute. However, the certainty and precision of laws are essential principles of our legal system. They allow ordinary people to understand when their behaviour might become criminal. As a matter of principle, it is for parliament to ensure that the laws it passes are clear enough to be applied consistently and, more importantly, predictably.

During the bill's second reading, Conservative MP Alex Chalk argued that, while it's currently possible to prosecute someone who downloads material like a bomb-making manual, streaming and making notes of the same information would fall outside of the law. However, such a case would come under existing section 58 laws, which makes it an offence to 'make a record' of material likely to be useful to a terrorist.

> ## *'It is for parliament to ensure that the laws it passes are clear enough to be applied consistently and, more importantly, predictably.'*

It is possible that, in some cases, viewing this material could indicate what the Government calls a 'pattern of behaviour'. In other words, it could suggest that the person is interested in (if not sympathetic towards) terrorist causes. But without evidence that the person wants to go that step further, there's the risk of criminalising mere thoughts.

The French example

The difficulties in passing legislation of this kind have been explored by the French Parliament. Previously, France tried to make it a criminal offence to 'habitually' access websites that supported or called for acts of terrorism, unless there were 'legitimate reasons,' such as journalistic or academic research.

This was struck down by the French Constitutional Court, which ruled that the law violated free speech and the freedom to communicate ideas and opinions. It also found the laws were not clear or certain enough. In fact, the French version was more specific than proposed British laws, as it was aimed at terrorist websites, rather than anything which could help commit terrorist acts. If the French example is anything to go by, the new laws are a cause for concern.

Are our rights being protected?

It's vital that there are enough safeguards in place to protect people who are acting without malicious intentions. The defence of 'reasonable excuse' is one important protection in the proposals. This defence would probably be available for academics and journalists. However, someone would already have been arrested, kept in custody, interviewed under caution, and put in the dock before they could use this defence before a jury. It's an important safeguard, but one that arguably comes too late in the process.

One potential solution is to amend the legislation to include the requirement that a person be acting with a criminal or terrorist intent. This would include cases that Alex Chalk MP refers to, where someone is accessing material with a view to cause harm, but excludes those who look mistakenly or out of curiosity. If the Government is serious about striking the right balance between liberty and security, the offence should include a criminal intent or be withdrawn altogether.

29 June 2018

The war on terror continues and still no one counts the costs

By Kenan Malik

The war on terror. A phrase forever in the media and on our lips. Its very ubiquity helps obscure the reality of that war.

America, according to a new study from Brown University, is running counter-terror operations in 76 countries – 39% of all the nations in the world.

Since 2001, at least half-a-million people have been killed in wars in Afghanistan, Pakistan and Iraq alone. The real figure is likely to be far higher.

A *New York Times* investigation last year suggested that the civilian toll in Iraq from coalition airstrikes could be 31 times greater than officially admitted.

Include the conflicts in Libya, Syria and Yemen and the toll would be significantly higher still.

These are just direct deaths. The number of indirect deaths – from the destruction of health facilities or infrastructure – run into the millions. Meanwhile, the *2017 Global Terrorism Index* suggested that terrorist attacks accounted for 25,000 deaths in just the previous year. Up to 106 countries, more than half the nations in the world, suffered deadly attacks, 94% of which were in Africa, Asia and the Middle East.

The level of terrorism is usually the justification for the intensity of the war on terror. Yet, despite the effective destruction of Islamic State, the influence and scope of terror groups is greater now than it was in 2001. Already this year, the US has dropped more bombs on Afghanistan than in any previous year. The Taliban still controls 20% of the country and its bloodlust remains undiminished. Just last week, a suicide bomber killed at least 53 people in Kabul.

What began after 9/11 as an attempt to eliminate al-Qaida has metastasised into a never-ending war against an ever-expanding universe of terror groups. And yet it's become little more than background noise in the West. Isn't it time we started asking serious questions about the war on terror, its scope and its consequences?

25 November 2018

Key facts

- The most famous incident in early modern history is probably the gunpowder plot of 1605 when Guy Fawkes attempted to blow up the House of Lords. (page 7)

- In the second half of the 19th century, European anarchism introduced the idea of 'propaganda by deed' as a tactic of anti-government resistance (page 7)

- The heavy death toll of the Great Famine in Ireland from 1846 to 1852 prompted calls for Irish home rule and resulted in the formation of networks of radical revolutionaries, the Fenians. (page 7)

- In 1909, the Indian revolutionary Madan Lal Dhingra assassinated a British official on the steps of the Imperial Institute in London. This followed a number of assassinations and bombings in India, as militant networks of anti-colonial radicals attempted to destabilise British imperial rule by initiating a 'reign of terror'. (page 7)

- The majority of people arrested for terrorism-related offences in Great Britain since 11 September 2001 have been British nationals: 58% of people declared they were a British national at the time of their arrest. (page 8)

- There were 273 arrests for terrorism-related activity in the year ending 31 December 2018, a decrease of 41% compared with the 465 arrests in the previous year. (page 10)

- As at 31 December 2018, there were 221 persons in custody in Great Britain for terrorism-related offences, a decrease of 1% on the 224 persons in the previous year. (page 10)

- Of those in custody, the majority (79%) were categorised as holding Islamist-extremist views, a further 13% as holding far right-wing ideologies and 8% other ideologies. (page 10)

- The Terrorism Act 2000, allows the police to hold people arrested for terrorism offences for a period of seven days and grants them the authority to stop and search a person/vehicle without suspicion if they're operating in a designated area. (page 12)

- The IRA ceasefire in 1994 was the event that triggered anti-terrorism action. (page 12)

- In 2017, 62 people were killed in 33 religiously inspired terrorist attacks in the EU, compared to 135 deaths in 13 attacks in 2016, according to Europol figures. (page 13)

- The four terrorist groups responsible for the most deaths in 2017 were the Islamic State of Iraq and the Levant (ISIL), the Taliban, Al-Shabaab and Boko Haram. These four groups were responsible for 10,632 deaths from terrorism, representing 56.5% of total deaths in 2017. (page 14)

- The past decade has experienced the largest surge in terrorist activity in the past fifty years. (page 14)

- The Islamic State of Iraq and the Levant, often referred to as ISIL, ISIS or Daesh, was the most active terrorist organisation in 2017, a position it has held since 2015. (page 14)

- The Taliban emerged in Afghanistan in 1994 as a reactionary group that combined both mujahideen that had previously fought against the 1979 Soviet invasion, and groups of Pashtun tribesmen. The Taliban took control of Afghanistan in 1996. (page 14)

- Al-Shabaab, a Salafist militant group active in East Africa, first emerged in a battle over Somalia's capital in the summer of 2006. (page 15)

- In 2016/17, a total of 6,093 individuals were referred due to concerns that they were vulnerable to being drawn into terrorism. 1,976 of those were referred via the education sector. (page 19)

- The world's first suicide bomber was a Russian revolutionary named Ignaty Grinevitsky. He was a member of the People's Will, a terrorist organisation which had tried and failed on many occasions to assassinate Tsar Alexander II, the leader of Imperial Russia. (page 20)

- The Prevent strategy forms part of the Government's wider counter-terrorism strategy, known as CONTEST. (page 33)

- The Channel programme in England and Wales is a voluntary initiative that provides a multi-agency approach to support people vulnerable to being drawn into terrorism. (page 33)

The 7/7 bombings

Also know as the London bombings, this refers to the events of 7 July 2005, when four suicide bombers took the lives of 56 people on the London transport system. The incident was the deadliest single act of terrorism in the UK since Lockerbie (the 1988 bombing of Pan Am Flight 103 which killed 270), and the deadliest bombing in London since the Second World War. The attacks were significant in drawing UK attention to the terrorism problem - they demonstrated that terrorism could occur at home as well as abroad, and could even be perpetrated by British citizens (three of the four bombers were British).

Al-Qaeda

A group/organisation of Islamic militants, responsible for the 9/11 attacks in America.

Atheism

Atheism refers to the firm belief that there is no god or divine power at work in the universe, and human beings are constrained to one life only, with no continued existence after death.

Counter-terrorism

Counter-terrorism refers to the tactics and techniques used by governments and other groups to prevent or minimise a terrorist threat.

Extremism

Extremism refers to beliefs or practices that are seen as radical, and can give rise to militance. Groups justifying their violence on Islamic grounds, such as Al-Qaeda.

The Human Rights Act

The Human Rights Act is a written law (statute) passed in 1998 which is in force in England and Wales. The rights that are protected by this law are based on the articles of the European Convention on Human Rights. There is an ongoing debate between supporters of the Act and its critics as to whether it should be kept, or replaced with a new UK Bill of Rights.

ISIS

ISIS stands for 'the Islamic State of Iraq and al-Sham'. It is an extreme jihadi group that now controls a large territory in western Iraq and eastern Syria.

Islam

Islam is the second largest faith group in the UK today - 2.8% of the UK population were Muslims in 2001, according to the last census. Muslims believe in the word of Allah (God) as set out in their holy book, the Quran, by the prophet Muhammed in Arabia 1,300 years ago. Islam is a way of life, and followers must observe strict rules regarding diet, lifestyle and worship.

Radicalisation

The process by which a person, or group of people, adopt extreme religious, political or ideological beliefs.

September eleventh (9/11)

9/11 is a common way of referring to the events of 11 September 2001, the date on which four passenger planes were hijacked by Al-Qaeda militants and flown into US targets - notably the twin towers of the World Trade Center in New York - causing thousands of lives to be lost. These attacks were significant in bringing terrorism into the international spotlight, changing the world's political climate and launching the 'War on Terror'.

Terrorism

The word 'terrorism' dates back to the 18th century, but there is no globally accepted definition of the term. The most widely accepted is probably that put forward by the US State Department, which states that terrorism is 'premeditated, politically motivated violence perpetrated against non-combatant targets by subnational groups or clandestine agents, usually intended to influence an audience.' Types include Nationalist-Separatist, Religious, Right-Wing and Left-Wing Terrorism.

The Taliban

A militant Islamist group which ruled large parts of Afghanistan between 1996 and 2001.

Treason

The crime of betraying one's country.

Violent extremism

When violence is used to achieve or promote radical/extreme religious, political or ideological beliefs.

Assignments

Brainstorming

- In small groups, discuss what you know about terrorism and extremism. Consider the following?

  - What is terrorism?

  - What is extremism?

  - What is the difference between terrorism and extremism?

  - What is the earliest memory you have of learning about a terrorist attack, either through broadcast, print or social media?

Research

- Do some research about recent terrorist attacks from around the world. Choose an event from the last three years and write some notes about what happened, the cause and the effects. Share with your class.

- With a partner, do some research about US anti-terror laws. Referring to the article about the Terrorism Act 2000 on page 12, compare UK anti-terror legislation with that of the US. What are the similarities/differences? Share your findings with the rest of the class.

- In pairs, research the current threat levels in the UK from both domestic and international terrorism.

  - How are these threat levels decided?

  - Which groups are most strongly linked to terrorist activity in the UK and abroad?

  - What are these groups trying to achieve?

  - What is the UK Government's current strategy to combat these threats?

Design

- Design a poster that could be displayed in public places to demonstrate what members of the public should do if they suspect someone they know is involved in terrorism or violent extremism.

- Referring to the article on page 19, think about the factors that can make someone vulnerable to radicalisation by a terrorist organisation. Create a leaflet that gives help and advice to family members who are worried that a son/daughter, friend or relative are affected.

- Create an infographic timeline showing key periods of terrorism in history. Use illustrations, photographs and key facts from each period.

Oral

- 'Right-wing extremist violence is our biggest threat.' Debate this statement in small groups, then write down your main thoughts/comments and share with the rest of your class.

- 'One man's terrorist is another man's freedom fighter.' Discuss your views on the meaning behind this phrase and summarise your thoughts in the form of an essay, referring to at least two historical or current figures in your answer: for example, Yasser Arafat, Nelson Mandela, Gerry Adams.

- Choose one of the illustrations in this book and, in pairs, discuss what you think the artist was trying to portray with their image.

- In small groups, discuss the different attack methods used by terrorist organisations. What motivates someone to become a suicide terrorist?

- ISIS bride Shamima Begum has received a lot of media attention recently. Opinion is divided on whether or not she should be allowed to return to the UK. Discuss as a class the reasons for both sides of the argument.

- In small groups, discuss where you think terrorists get their money and weapons from?

- As a class, discuss peace processes. Can you give some examples of peace processes that have put a stop to terrorist activities - either domestically or globally?

Reading/writing

- Write a one-paragraph definition of each of the following types of terrorism:

  - Jihadist

  - Right-wing

  - Left-wing

  - Religious

- Do some research on non-violent extremists. Can you give some examples of current or historical figures who could fit this description?

- Read the article *Terrorism in Britain: a brief history* on page 7. Choose one the events noted in the piece and write your own article covering it in the style of a current newspaper.

- Read *My Sister Lives on the Mantelpiece* by Annabel Pitcher (2011). Write a single paragraph review of the book.

Acknowledgements

The publisher is grateful for permission to reproduce the material in this book. While every care has been taken to trace and acknowledge copyright, the publisher tenders its apology for any accidental infringement or where copyright has proved untraceable. The publisher would be pleased to come to a suitable arrangement in any such case with the rightful owner.

Images

All images courtesy of iStock except page 6: Freepik, pages 1, 22, 27, 34, 36: Pixabay, page 20: rawpixel.com and pages 24, 29, 30, 31, 32, 38, 39: Unsplash

Illustrations

Don Hatcher: pages 19 & 23. Simon Kneebone: pages 26 & 37. Angelo Madrid: pages 3 & 7.

Additional acknowledgements

With thanks to the Independence team: Shelley Baldry, Danielle Lobban, Jackie Staines and Jan Sunderland.

Tracy Biram

Cambridge, May 2019